POPPIN'
FRESH ®
HOMEMADE
COOKIES

D0235156

Ottenheimer Publishers, Inc.

Managing Editor: Diane B. Anderson
Associate Editor: Elaine Christiansen
Senior Food Editor: Jackie Sheehan
Test Kitchen Coordinator: Pat Peterson
Circulation Specialist: Karen Goodsell
Food Editor and Food Stylist: Sharon Harding
Contributing Editor: Patricia Miller
Home Economists: Pillsbury Publications
Nutrition Coordinator: Patricia Godfrey, R.D.
Design, Production: Hedstrom/Blessing, Inc.
Photography: Hedstrom/Blessing Photo

This edition published by arrangement
with Ottenheimer Publishers, Inc.,
distributed by Wholesale Warehousing Industries, Inc.,
250 Granton Drive, Richmond Hill, Ontario, Canada, L4B 1H7.

Cover Photo: Chocolate Chip Cookies
Variation—Kid-Sized Cookies p. 31.

CONTENTS

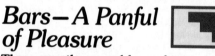

How we love cookies! Whether quick and easy drop cookies, cutouts to suit the season, shaped cookies or cut into bars, there is a favorite for everyone! With creative flair, triple-tested recipes and timely tips, this cookbook offers you a delightful opportunity for pleasant baking and delicious eating.

Baking Perfect Cookies Every Time

To help you make this selection of Poppin' Fresh® Homemade Cookies turn out just right:

- **Choose either margarine or butter**—they're interchangeable. Although there are diet and whipped products on the market, our recipes have been tested with regular margarine and butter and we recommend these for successful results.

- **Brown sugar should be firmly packed** so that it holds its shape when turned out of the measuring cup. Break up any lumps for they'll melt and create holes in your cookies. To keep brown sugar moist, store it in a tightly covered container in a cool place. If it does harden:
  - heat it in a 250° to 300°F. oven for a few minutes. Use immediately before it hardens again.
  - or in a microwave oven on HIGH, bring ½ cup water in a microwave-safe cup to a boil. Put brown sugar in microwave-safe container and place it near the water. Microwave on HIGH for 1½ to 2½ minutes for a half pound of brown sugar or until soft.

- **Use large eggs.** Our recipe testing is done with this size.

- **Measure ingredients with standard measuring cups and spoons.**

- **Heat the oven for 10 to 15 minutes** to reach baking temperature before beginning to bake.

- **Select cookie sheets that have a small rim on one or both ends,** not on all four sides.

- **Shiny pans are best for light, even browning** and were used to test these recipes.

- **Place cookie sheet in oven with at least two inches of clearance on all sides** for best air circulation in the oven. Baking one sheet of cookies at a time provides the best air circulation in the oven, but if you bake two at a time, leave one inch of air space on all sides of both sheets.

- **Remove cookies from sheets with a metal spatula or turner.** If cookies remain on the sheets for too long, they may harden and stick. Should this occur, put the sheets back in the oven for one minute.

- **Cool cookie sheets between bakings.** Hot sheets will cause the fat in the dough to melt before baking, resulting in flat cookies. If necessary, wipe sheets with paper towels between bakings. Grease cookie sheets only if recipe calls for it to avoid excess spreading.

- **Cool cookies completely in a single layer before stacking or storing.** Cooling cookies on wire racks allows air to circulate around them; steam evaporates and prevents the cookies from becoming soggy. **Bar cookies should be cooled in the baking pan on a wire rack.**

Keeping Cookies Fresh and Flavorful

- To prevent flavors from mixing, **store each kind of cookie in a separate container.**
  - **To keep soft cookies soft, store in a container with a tight-fitting cover.** Place sheets of waxed paper between layers so cookies won't stick together.
    - **To keep crisp cookies crisp, store in a container with a loose-fitting cover.** However, if you live in a humid climate, containers should be tightly covered.
      - **To store bars, place in a tightly-covered container or leave them right in the baking pan.** Cover the pan with foil, plastic wrap, or slip it into a plastic bag.

Packing to Keep Cookies from Becoming Crumbs

There's nothing like receiving a package of cookies from home.

- **Choose cookies that can withstand the trip.** Bars, crisp and crunchy, or soft and moist drop cookies travel well.
- **Use a strong cardboard box or metal container** covered with gift wrap or contact paper.
- **Line the cookie container** with plastic wrap, waxed paper or aluminum foil. **Cushion cookies** with crumpled waxed paper on the bottom and top.
- If necessary because of variety, **wrap cookies individually or in back-to-back pairs** in plastic wrap, **or in groups** in plastic bags.
- **Pack snugly in rows.** Tuck shredded paper or crushed waxed paper into the holes to prevent jiggling. Protect each layer with waxed paper or paper towels.
- **Mark the box "perishable"** to encourage careful handling.

Freezing's a Snap

For best results when making extra batches to freeze:

- **Freeze each kind of cookie separately** to keep flavors from mingling.
- **Use plastic bags** for a small number of cookies; **use cans or plastic freezer containers with tight-fitting lids** for a larger number of cookies. Cardboard boxes are not recommended. Cookies will dry out and may absorb undesirable flavors from the cardboard.
- **Layer glazed or frosted cookies between sheets of waxed paper** after glaze or frosting is firm. Thaw in a single layer to prevent sticking. Or, freeze these cookies without frosting, then thaw, frost and serve.
- **Wrap bars in packets** of four, eight or a convenient number, **or freeze them in plastic containers.**
- **Just about all cookies**, except meringues, **freeze well** up to six months.

Giving Cookies as Gifts

From the earliest days of this country, Americans have been giving cookies as gifts. Try some of these packaging ideas for cookies you share:

- **Use decorative paper sacks or freezer bags**, and tie with colorful ribbons.
- **Decorate coffee or shortening cans** with wrapping or contact paper.
- Pack cookies in a **wide-mouth canning jar.** Cover the lid with fabric and secure it by screwing on the outer ring.
- Weave ribbons through **fruit or vegetable baskets lined with cellophane** or plastic wrap for a more festive look.
- **Purchase decorated tins.**

So now you're set. Thumb through this selection of Poppin' Fresh® Homemade Cookie recipes and choose one that fits your mood or the occasion. It's a time-honored way of saying "I love you" with something from the oven.

POPPIN' FRESH® HOMEMADE COOKIES

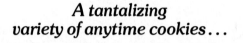

Cookie Jar COOKIES

A tantalizing variety of anytime cookies...

A full cookie jar is a tantalizing temptation, especially when it's well-stocked with cookies like these. They're ideal for snacking, for packing in lunches, for grabbing on the run, for dunking in milk, or for mailing to students away at college. These aren't dainty tea cookies, these are the hearty variety. They're chock-full of good things to eat, like almonds, macadamia nuts, pecans, cashews, dates, raisins, coconut, sunflower seeds, peanut butter, and oatmeal. They're spiced with cinnamon, ginger, cloves, nutmeg and anise. But best of all, they're just plain good to eat.

Variety is these cookies' middle name. **Almond Cookie Cakes** can be made with egg substitutes for those who are trying to cut down on their cholesterol intake. **Crispy Corn Chip Munchies** are almost cracker-like and, as their name implies, are made with crushed corn chips. Potato flakes are the secret ingredient in **Lemon-Go-Lightly Cookies**. Licorice lovers will fall for **Licorice Snaps**, buttery refrigerator cookies with the distinctive taste of anise.

Three cookies are energy-packed to perk up drooping daughters,

flagging fathers, and sagging sons. **Nutritious Poppin' Fresh® Cookies** combine rolled oats, chocolate chips, sunflower seeds, and your choice of peanut butter, wheat germ and coconut in cookies ideal for lunch boxes. **Peanut Butter Banana Drops** blend peanut butter, bananas and rolled oats in a wholesome combination. **Chewy Date Bran Macaroons** team up oat bran with dates and nuts for a perfect picker-upper.

When you want cookies that melt in your mouth, give **Cashew Shortbread Squares** a try. Cashews provide a variation on these cookies that call the moors of Scotland home. Chocoholics will devour **Chocolate Ginger Zebras** with their white chocolate drizzle and **Chocolate Macadamia Cookies with White Chocolate Chunks**. What could be better than delectable macadamia nuts and chunks of white chocolate studding a dark chocolate cookie?

In 1955, **Caramel Cream Sandwich Cookies** won the sixth Pillsbury Bake-Off® Contest. The judges loved them then and you're sure to now.

Pictured on previous page: Oatmeal Carrot Cookies and Cranberry Cookies

Freshly grated carrots add interesting appeal to these soft and chewy oatmeal cookies.

Oatmeal Carrot Cookies

1 cup Pillsbury's BEST® All Purpose or Unbleached Flour
1 cup quick-cooking rolled oats
1 teaspoon baking powder
¼ teaspoon baking soda
½ cup margarine or butter, softened
½ cup honey
1 teaspoon vanilla
1 egg
½ cup chopped nuts
½ cup (1 medium) shredded carrot

Heat oven to 350°F. Grease cookie sheets. Lightly spoon flour into measuring cup; level off. In large bowl, combine flour, rolled oats, baking powder, baking soda, margarine, honey, vanilla and egg at low speed until well blended. Stir in nuts and carrot. Drop by rounded teaspoonfuls 2 inches apart onto greased cookie sheets. Bake at 350°F for 8 to 12 minutes or until edges are light golden brown. Immediately remove from cookie sheets. 2½ to 3 dozen cookies.

HIGH ALTITUDE — Above 3500 Feet: No change.

NUTRITION INFORMATION PER SERVING

SERVING SIZE: 1 COOKIE		PERCENT U.S. RDA PER SERVING	
CALORIES	80	PROTEIN	*
PROTEIN	1g	VITAMIN A	10%
CARBOHYDRATE	9g	VITAMIN C	*
FAT	4g	THIAMINE	2%
CHOLESTEROL	8mg	RIBOFLAVIN	*
SODIUM	50mg	NIACIN	*
POTASSIUM	30mg	CALCIUM	*
		IRON	*

*Contains less than 2% of the U.S. RDA of this nutrient.

Tart and tangy cranberries accent these nutty, soft-textured drop cookies. They're a great cookie for the holidays.

Cranberry Cookies

½ cup sugar
½ cup firmly packed brown sugar
¼ cup margarine or butter, softened
2 tablespoons milk
1 tablespoon lemon juice
½ teaspoon vanilla
1 egg
1½ cups Pillsbury's BEST® All Purpose or Unbleached Flour
½ teaspoon baking powder
¼ teaspoon baking soda
¼ teaspoon salt
1 cup fresh or frozen cranberries, coarsely chopped
½ cup chopped nuts

Heat oven to 375°F. Grease cookie sheets. In large bowl, combine sugar, brown sugar and margarine; beat well. Add milk, lemon juice, vanilla and egg; blend well. Lightly spoon flour into measuring cup; level off. Stir in flour, baking powder, baking soda and salt; mix well. Stir in cranberries and nuts. Drop by rounded teaspoonfuls 2 inches apart onto greased cookie sheets. Bake at 375°F. for 8 to 12 minutes or until edges are light golden brown. Immediately remove from cookie sheets. 3 dozen cookies.

HIGH ALTITUDE — Above 3500 Feet: Increase flour to 2 cups. Bake as directed above.

NUTRITION INFORMATION PER SERVING

SERVING SIZE: 1 COOKIE		PERCENT U.S. RDA PER SERVING	
CALORIES	70	PROTEIN	*
PROTEIN	1g	VITAMIN A	*
CARBOHYDRATE	10g	VITAMIN C	*
FAT	3g	THIAMINE	2%
CHOLESTEROL	8mg	RIBOFLAVIN	*
SODIUM	45mg	NIACIN	*
POTASSIUM	30mg	CALCIUM	*
		IRON	2%

*Contains less than 2% of the U.S. RDA of this nutrient.

POPPIN' FRESH® HOMEMADE COOKIES

These rich butter cookies with delicate caramel flavor are a prize-winning recipe from the 6th Bake-Off® contest held in 1955.

Caramel Cream Sandwich Cookies

COOKIES
¾ cup firmly packed brown sugar
1 cup butter, softened
1 egg yolk
2 cups Pillsbury's BEST® All
    Purpose or Unbleached Flour

FROSTING
2 tablespoons butter
1¼ cups powdered sugar
½ teaspoon vanilla
4 to 5 teaspoons milk

In large bowl, beat brown sugar and 1 cup butter until light and fluffy. Add egg yolk; blend well. Lightly spoon flour into measuring cup; level off. Stir in flour; mix well. Cover with plastic wrap; refrigerate 15 minutes if necessary for easier handling.

Heat oven to 325°F. Shape dough into 1-inch balls. Place 2 inches apart on ungreased cookie sheets. Flatten to 1½-inch circle with fork dipped in flour. Bake at 325°F. for 10 to 14 minutes or until light golden brown. Immediately remove from cookie sheets; cool completely.

Heat 2 tablespoons butter in medium saucepan over medium heat until light golden brown. Remove from heat. Stir in remaining frosting ingredients, adding enough milk until frosting is of desired spreading consistency; blend until smooth. Spread 1 teaspoon frosting between 2 cooled cookies. Repeat with remaining frosting and cookies.*
2½ dozen sandwich cookies.

TIP: *If frosting becomes too stiff as it cools, add enough additional milk until frosting is of desired spreading consistency.

HIGH ALTITUDE—Above 3500 Feet: No change.

NUTRITION INFORMATION PER SERVING
SERVING SIZE:
1 SANDWICH COOKIE

		PERCENT U.S. RDA
		PER SERVING
CALORIES	130	PROTEIN .... *
PROTEIN	1g	VITAMIN A 4%
CARBOHYDRATE	16g	VITAMIN C .... *
FAT	7g	THIAMINE 2%
CHOLESTEROL	25mg	RIBOFLAVIN 2%
SODIUM	70mg	NIACIN 2%
POTASSIUM	30mg	CALCIUM .... *
		IRON 2%

*Contains less than 2% of the U.S. RDA of this nutrient.

Caramel Cream Sandwich Cookies

Potato flakes are the secret ingredient in these chewy, delicately flavored cookies.

Lemon-Go-Lightly Cookies

- 2 cups Pillsbury's BEST® All Purpose or Unbleached Flour
- 2 cups Hungry Jack® Mashed Potato Flakes
- 1 cup sugar
- 1 cup firmly packed brown sugar
- ½ to ¾ cup finely chopped nuts
- 1 teaspoon baking soda
- ¾ cup margarine or butter, melted
- 1 teaspoon grated lemon peel
- 2 eggs
- ¼ cup sugar

Heat oven to 350°F. Lightly spoon flour into measuring cup; level off. In large bowl, combine all ingredients except ¼ cup sugar; blend well. (Mixture will be crumbly.) Firmly press into 1-inch balls; roll in ¼ cup sugar. Place 2 inches apart on ungreased cookie sheets. Bake at 350°F. for 9 to 12 minutes or until golden brown. Cool 1 minute; remove from cookie sheets. 6 dozen cookies.

HIGH ALTITUDE — Above 3500 Feet: No change.

NUTRITION INFORMATION PER SERVING

SERVING SIZE: 1 COOKIE		PERCENT U.S. RDA PER SERVING	
CALORIES	70	PROTEIN	°
PROTEIN	1g	VITAMIN A	°
CARBOHYDRATE	11g	VITAMIN C	°
FAT	3g	THIAMINE	2%
CHOLESTEROL	8mg	RIBOFLAVIN	°
SODIUM	45mg	NIACIN	°
POTASSIUM	45mg	CALCIUM	°
		IRON	°

° Contains less than 2% of the U.S. RDA of this nutrient.

Mix and shape, then slice and bake these uniquely flavored cookies. Anise seed gives them their distinctive licorice flavor.

Licorice Snaps

- ¾ cup sugar
- ¾ cup firmly packed brown sugar
- 1 cup margarine or butter, softened
- 1 egg
- 2 cups Pillsbury's BEST® All Purpose or Unbleached Flour
- 1 tablespoon anise seed
- 1 teaspoon baking soda
- ½ teaspoon salt
- ½ teaspoon cloves
- ½ teaspoon cinnamon
- ½ cup chopped pecans

In large bowl, beat sugar, brown sugar and margarine until light and fluffy. Add egg; blend well. Lightly spoon flour into measuring cup; level off. Stir in flour, anise seed, baking soda, salt, cloves and cinnamon; mix well. Stir in pecans. Cover with plastic wrap; refrigerate 30 minutes if necessary for easier handling. Divide dough in half on 2 sheets of waxed paper; shape each half into 10-inch roll. Wrap; refrigerate 4 hours or overnight.

Heat oven to 375°F. Cut dough into ¼-inch slices. Place 1 inch apart on ungreased cookie sheets. Bake at 375°F. for 6 to 8 minutes or until light golden brown. Immediately remove from cookie sheets. 6 to 6½ dozen cookies.

HIGH ALTITUDE — Above 3500 Feet: Increase flour to 2¼ cups. Bake as directed above.

NUTRITION INFORMATION PER SERVING

SERVING SIZE: 1 COOKIE		PERCENT U.S. RDA PER SERVING	
CALORIES	60	PROTEIN	°
PROTEIN	1g	VITAMIN A	2%
CARBOHYDRATE	7g	VITAMIN C	°
FAT	3g	THIAMINE	°
CHOLESTEROL	2mg	RIBOFLAVIN	°
SODIUM	55mg	NIACIN	°
POTASSIUM	15mg	CALCIUM	°
		IRON	°

° Contains less than 2% of the U.S. RDA of this nutrient.

Each of these soft-textured cookies is like a tiny bite of apple cake.

Applesauce Cookies

1 cup sugar
½ cup shortening
1¼ cups unsweetened applesauce
1 egg
2½ cups Pillsbury's BEST® All Purpose or Unbleached Flour
1 teaspoon baking soda
1 teaspoon cinnamon
¼ teaspoon cloves
¼ teaspoon salt
1 cup raisins
½ cup chopped nuts

Heat oven to 375°F. Grease cookie sheets. In large bowl, beat sugar and shortening until light and fluffy. Add applesauce and egg; blend well. Lightly spoon flour into measuring cup; level off. Stir in flour, baking soda, cinnamon, cloves and salt; mix well. Stir in raisins and nuts. Drop by rounded tablespoonfuls 2 inches apart onto greased cookie sheets. Bake at 375°F. for 11 to 16 minutes or until light golden brown. Immediately remove from cookie sheets. 3 dozen cookies.

HIGH ALTITUDE—Above 3500 Feet: No change.

NUTRITION INFORMATION PER SERVING

SERVING SIZE: 1 COOKIE

		PERCENT U.S. RDA PER SERVING	
CALORIES	110	PROTEIN	2%
PROTEIN	1g	VITAMIN A	*
CARBOHYDRATE	17g	VITAMIN C	*
FAT	4g	THIAMINE	4%
CHOLESTEROL	8mg	RIBOFLAVIN	2%
SODIUM	50mg	NIACIN	2%
POTASSIUM	55mg	CALCIUM	*
		IRON	2%

*Contains less than 2% of the U.S. RDA of this nutrient.

This crispy cinnamon cookie is great for dunking!

Cinnamon and Sugar Crispies

¾ cup sugar
¾ cup margarine or butter, softened
1 egg
2 cups Pillsbury's BEST® All Purpose or Unbleached Flour
1 teaspoon cinnamon
2 tablespoons sugar
1 teaspoon cinnamon

In large bowl, beat ¾ cup sugar and margarine until light and fluffy. Add egg; blend well. Lightly spoon flour into measuring cup; level off. Stir in flour and 1 teaspoon cinnamon; mix well. Cover with plastic wrap; refrigerate 30 minutes if necessary for easier handling.

Heat oven to 350°F. In small bowl, combine 2 tablespoons sugar and 1 teaspoon cinnamon. Shape dough into 1¼-inch balls; roll in sugar-cinnamon mixture. Place 2 inches apart on ungreased cookie sheets. Flatten with bottom of glass. Bake at 350°F. for 10 to 12 minutes or until edges are light golden brown. Immediately remove from cookie sheets. 3½ to 4 dozen cookies.

HIGH ALTITUDE—Above 3500 Feet: No change.

NUTRITION INFORMATION PER SERVING

SERVING SIZE: 1 COOKIE

		PERCENT U.S. RDA PER SERVING	
CALORIES	60	PROTEIN	*
PROTEIN	1g	VITAMIN A	2%
CARBOHYDRATE	8g	VITAMIN C	*
FAT	3g	THIAMINE	2%
CHOLESTEROL	6mg	RIBOFLAVIN	*
SODIUM	35mg	NIACIN	*
POTASSIUM	10mg	CALCIUM	*
		IRON	*

*Contains less than 2% of the U.S. RDA of this nutrient.

COOKIE JAR COOKIES

POPPIN' FRESH® HOMEMADE COOKIES

Chunks of creamy white chocolate and mouth-watering macadamia nuts are scattered throughout these irresistible dark chocolate cookies.

Chocolate Macadamia Cookies with White Chocolate Chunks

¾ cup firmly packed brown sugar
½ cup sugar
1 cup margarine or butter, softened
1 teaspoon almond extract
1 egg
2 cups Pillsbury's BEST® All Purpose or Unbleached Flour
¼ cup unsweetened cocoa
1 teaspoon baking soda
½ teaspoon salt
6-oz. white baking bar, cut into ½-inch chunks, or 1 cup vanilla milk chips*
3½-oz. jar macadamia nuts, coarsely chopped

Heat oven to 375°F. In large bowl, beat brown sugar, sugar and margarine until light and fluffy. Add almond extract and egg; blend well. Lightly spoon flour into measuring cup; level off. Stir in flour, cocoa, baking soda and salt; mix well. Stir in remaining ingredients. Drop by rounded tablespoonfuls 2 inches apart onto ungreased cookie sheets. Bake at 375°F. for 8 to 12 minutes or until set. Cool 1 minute; remove from cookie sheets. 2½ to 3 dozen cookies.

TIP: *If baking bar is difficult to cut, place in microwave-safe bowl and microwave on MEDIUM for 10 seconds.

HIGH ALTITUDE—Above 3500 Feet: Increase flour to 2 cups plus 3 tablespoons. Bake as directed above.

NUTRITION INFORMATION PER SERVING

SERVING SIZE: 1 COOKIE		PERCENT U.S. RDA PER SERVING	
CALORIES	150	PROTEIN	2%
PROTEIN	2g	VITAMIN A	4%
CARBOHYDRATE	16g	VITAMIN C	*
FAT	9g	THIAMINE	4%
CHOLESTEROL	8mg	RIBOFLAVIN	2%
SODIUM	130mg	NIACIN	2%
POTASSIUM	55mg	CALCIUM	2%
		IRON	2%

*Contains less than 2% of the U.S. RDA of this nutrient.

"Sugar and spice and everything nice" are baked into these crisp chocolate cookies with a white chocolate drizzle.

Chocolate Ginger Zebras

¼ cup sugar
⅓ cup shortening
¼ cup unsweetened cocoa
¼ cup dark corn syrup
2 tablespoons milk
1 egg
1½ cups Pillsbury's BEST® All Purpose or Unbleached Flour
½ teaspoon baking soda
½ teaspoon baking powder
½ teaspoon ginger
½ teaspoon cinnamon
⅛ teaspoon cloves
3 oz. vanilla-flavored candy coating
2 tablespoons shortening

Pictured on previous page: Chocolate Macadamia Cookies with White Chocolate Chunks and Chocolate Ginger Zebras

In large bowl, beat sugar and ⅓ cup shortening until light and fluffy. Add cocoa, corn syrup, milk and egg; blend well. Lightly spoon flour into measuring cup; level off. Stir in flour, baking soda, baking powder, ginger, cinnamon and cloves; mix well. Cover with plastic wrap; refrigerate 1½ to 2 hours for easier handling.

Heat oven to 350°F. Lightly grease cookie sheets. On floured surface, roll dough to ⅛-inch thickness. Cut with floured 2½ to 3-inch cookie cutter. Place 1 inch apart on greased cookie sheets. Bake at 350°F. for 6 to 9 minutes or until set. Immediately remove from cookie sheets. Cool.

In small saucepan, melt candy coating and 2 tablespoons shortening over low heat, stirring constantly. Drizzle over cooled cookies. Allow to set before storing. 2½ to 3 dozen cookies.

HIGH ALTITUDE—Above 3500 Feet: Increase flour to 1½ cups plus 1 tablespoon. Bake as directed above.

NUTRITION INFORMATION PER SERVING

SERVING SIZE: 1 COOKIE		PERCENT U.S. RDA PER SERVING	
CALORIES	70	PROTEIN	*
PROTEIN	1g	VITAMIN A	*
CARBOHYDRATE	9g	VITAMIN C	*
FAT	3g	THIAMINE	4%
CHOLESTEROL	8mg	RIBOFLAVIN	2%
SODIUM	30mg	NIACIN	*
POTASSIUM	15mg	CALCIUM	*
		IRON	2%

*Contains less than 2% of the U.S. RDA of this nutrient.

This chewy cookie is an excellent choice for lunch boxes and also a great cookie for mailing to that son or daughter who is away at school.

Lunch Box Crunch Cookies

½ cup sugar
½ cup firmly packed brown sugar
½ cup margarine or butter, softened
½ teaspoon vanilla
1 egg
1 cup Pillsbury's BEST® All Purpose or Unbleached Flour
1 cup rolled oats
½ cup shredded coconut
½ teaspoon baking soda
¼ teaspoon baking powder
¼ teaspoon salt
1 cup cornflakes cereal
½ cup chopped nuts

Heat oven to 350°F. In large bowl, beat sugar, brown sugar and margarine until light and fluffy. Add vanilla and egg; blend well. Lightly spoon flour into measuring cup; level off. Stir in flour, rolled oats, coconut, baking soda, baking powder and salt. Stir in cornflakes and nuts. Shape into 1-inch balls. Place 2 inches apart on ungreased cookie sheets. Bake at 350°F. for 8 to 12 minutes or until light golden brown. Immediately remove from cookie sheets. 4½ dozen cookies.

HIGH ALTITUDE—Above 3500 Feet: Increase flour to 1 cup plus 2 tablespoons. Bake as directed above.

NUTRITION INFORMATION PER SERVING

SERVING SIZE: 1 COOKIE		PERCENT U.S. RDA PER SERVING	
CALORIES	60	PROTEIN	*
PROTEIN	1g	VITAMIN A	*
CARBOHYDRATE	7g	VITAMIN C	*
FAT	3g	THIAMINE	2%
CHOLESTEROL	4mg	RIBOFLAVIN	*
SODIUM	50mg	NIACIN	*
POTASSIUM	25mg	CALCIUM	*
		IRON	*

*Contains less than 2% of the U.S. RDA of this nutrient.

Fill your cookie jar with these large crispy-chewy cookies. They are hearty, whole-some cookies perfect for the lunch box.

Nutritious Poppin' Fresh® Cookies

2¼ cups Pillsbury's BEST® All
  Purpose, Unbleached or
  Self-Rising Flour*
2 cups firmly packed brown sugar
1 teaspoon baking soda
½ teaspoon salt
1 cup margarine or butter,
  softened
2 teaspoons vanilla
2 eggs
2 cups quick-cooking rolled oats
½ cup chopped nuts or shelled
  sunflower seeds
6-oz. pkg. (1 cup) semi-sweet
  chocolate chips

Heat oven to 350°F. Lightly spoon flour into measuring cup; level off. In large bowl, combine flour, brown sugar, baking soda, salt, margarine, vanilla and eggs. Beat at medium speed until well blended, about 1 to 2 minutes. By hand, stir in rolled oats, nuts and chocolate chips. Drop by well rounded tablespoonfuls 2 inches apart onto un-greased cookie sheets. Bake at 350°F. for 12 to 15 minutes or until golden brown. Cool 1 minute; remove from cookie sheets. 28 cookies.

TIPS: *If using Pillsbury's BEST® Self-Rising Flour, omit soda and salt.

If desired, stir one of the following into the dough:
  1 cup peanut butter
  1 cup wheat germ
  1 cup flaked coconut
  1 cup instant nonfat dry milk

HIGH ALTITUDE—Above 3500 Feet: Increase flour to 2½ cups; decrease brown sugar to 1½ cups. Bake as directed above.

NUTRITION INFORMATION PER SERVING

SERVING SIZE: 1 COOKIE		PERCENT U.S. RDA PER SERVING	
CALORIES	230	PROTEIN	4%
PROTEIN	3g	VITAMIN A	6%
CARBOHYDRATE	31g	VITAMIN C	*
FAT	11g	THIAMINE	8%
CHOLESTEROL	20mg	RIBOFLAVIN	4%
SODIUM	160mg	NIACIN	4%
POTASSIUM	130mg	CALCIUM	2%
		IRON	8%

*Contains less than 2% of the U.S. RDA of this nutrient.

Nutritious Poppin' Fresh® Cookies

These tender cake-like cookies are full of crunchy pecans and sweet raisins. They are topped with a tangy orange glaze.

Orange-Pecan Cookies

1 cup sugar
1 cup margarine or butter, softened
2 eggs
3 cups Pillsbury's BEST® All Purpose or Unbleached Flour
1 teaspoon baking soda
½ teaspoon salt
6-oz. can frozen orange juice concentrate, thawed, reserving 3 tablespoons
½ cup chopped pecans
½ cup golden raisins
1 tablespoon water
Sugar

Heat oven to 375°F. In large bowl, combine 1 cup sugar, margarine and eggs; blend well. Lightly spoon flour into measuring cup; level off. In small bowl, combine flour, baking soda and salt. Alternately add dry ingredients and orange juice concentrate to sugar mixture, mixing well after each addition. Stir in pecans and raisins. Drop by teaspoonfuls 2 inches apart onto ungreased cookie sheets. Bake at 375°F. for 7 to 11 minutes or until light golden brown. Immediately remove from cookie sheets; place on wire racks.

In small bowl, combine reserved orange juice concentrate and water; brush over tops of cookies. Sprinkle with sugar. 5 dozen cookies.

HIGH ALTITUDE—Above 3500 Feet: Increase flour to 3¼ cups. Bake as directed above.

NUTRITION INFORMATION PER SERVING

SERVING SIZE: 1 COOKIE		PERCENT U.S. RDA PER SERVING	
CALORIES	80	PROTEIN	°
PROTEIN	1g	VITAMIN A	2%
CARBOHYDRATE	11g	VITAMIN C	8%
FAT	4g	THIAMINE	2%
CHOLESTEROL	8mg	RIBOFLAVIN	2%
SODIUM	75mg	NIACIN	*
POTASSIUM	45mg	CALCIUM	*
		IRON	2%

°Contains less than 2% of the U.S. RDA of this nutrient.

Delicious cashews complement these rich shortbread squares. They melt in your mouth!

Cashew Shortbread Squares

1¼ cups Pillsbury's BEST® All Purpose or Unbleached Flour
½ cup powdered sugar
¾ cup margarine or butter, softened
½ teaspoon vanilla
½ cup chopped unsalted or lightly salted cashews

Heat oven to 325°F. Lightly spoon flour into measuring cup; level off. In large bowl, combine flour, sugar, margarine and vanilla at low speed until dough forms. Stir in cashews. With floured hands, press dough out to form 9-inch square on ungreased cookie sheet. Bake at 325°F. for 20 to 28 minutes or until light golden brown. Immediately cut into thirty-six 1½-inch squares; remove from cookie sheet. 3 dozen cookies.

HIGH ALTITUDE—Above 3500 Feet: Increase flour to 1¼ cups plus 2 tablespoons. Bake as directed above.

NUTRITION INFORMATION PER SERVING

SERVING SIZE: 1 COOKIE		PERCENT U.S. RDA PER SERVING	
CALORIES	70	PROTEIN	°
PROTEIN	1g	VITAMIN A	2%
CARBOHYDRATE	5g	VITAMIN C	*
FAT	5g	THIAMINE	2%
CHOLESTEROL	0mg	RIBOFLAVIN	*
SODIUM	45mg	NIACIN	*
POTASSIUM	15mg	CALCIUM	*
		IRON	*

°Contains less than 2% of the U.S. RDA of this nutrient.

For a delightfully different, not-too-sweet treat, make a batch of these crispy, almost cracker-like cookies.

Crispy Corn Chip Munchies

½ cup sugar
1 cup margarine or butter, softened
1 teaspoon vanilla
1¾ cups Pillsbury's BEST® All
    Purpose or Unbleached Flour
1 cup finely crushed corn chips*
  Sugar

Heat oven to 350°F. In large bowl, beat sugar, margarine and vanilla until light and fluffy. Lightly spoon flour into measuring cup; level off. Stir in flour and corn chips; mix well. Drop by rounded teaspoonfuls 2 inches apart onto ungreased cookie sheets. Flatten with fork dipped in sugar. Bake at 350°F. for 10 to 15 minutes or until light golden brown. Immediately remove from cookie sheets. 3 dozen cookies.

TIP: *A food processor can be used to crush the corn chips. Or place them in a plastic bag; secure end and crush with a rolling pin.

HIGH ALTITUDE—Above 3500 Feet: Increase flour to 1¾ cups plus 1 tablespoon. Bake as directed above.

NUTRITION INFORMATION PER SERVING

SERVING SIZE: 1 COOKIE		PERCENT U.S. RDA PER SERVING	
CALORIES	90	PROTEIN	*
PROTEIN	1g	VITAMIN A	4%
CARBOHYDRATE	9g	VITAMIN C	*
FAT	6g	THIAMINE	2%
CHOLESTEROL	0mg	RIBOFLAVIN	*
SODIUM	70mg	NIACIN	*
POTASSIUM	10mg	CALCIUM	*
		IRON	*

*Contains less than 2% of the U.S. RDA of this nutrient.

A wholesome blend of ingredients makes these cookies ideal for between-meal cravings. Why not keep a supply in the cookie jar?

Peanut Butter Banana Drops

1 cup sugar
¾ cup chunky peanut butter
½ cup margarine or butter, softened
1 cup (2 to 3 medium) mashed
    bananas
2 teaspoons vanilla
3 eggs
1½ cups Pillsbury's BEST® All
    Purpose or Unbleached Flour
3 cups quick-cooking rolled oats
1 teaspoon baking soda
1 teaspoon cinnamon
½ teaspoon salt
  Powdered sugar

Heat oven to 350°F. Grease cookie sheets. In large bowl, beat sugar, peanut butter and margarine until light and fluffy. Add banana, vanilla and eggs; blend well. Lightly spoon flour into measuring cup; level off. Stir in flour, rolled oats, baking soda, cinnamon and salt; mix well. Drop by rounded teaspoonfuls 2 inches apart onto greased cookie sheets, flattening slightly with spoon. Bake at 350°F. for 8 to 14 minutes or until light golden brown. Immediately remove from cookie sheets. Cool. Sprinkle with powdered sugar. 5½ to 6 dozen cookies.

HIGH ALTITUDE—Above 3500 Feet: No change.

NUTRITION INFORMATION PER SERVING

SERVING SIZE: 1 COOKIE		PERCENT U.S. RDA PER SERVING	
CALORIES	70	PROTEIN	2%
PROTEIN	2g	VITAMIN A	*
CARBOHYDRATE	9g	VITAMIN C	*
FAT	3g	THIAMINE	2%
CHOLESTEROL	10mg	RIBOFLAVIN	*
SODIUM	60mg	NIACIN	2%
POTASSIUM	50mg	CALCIUM	*
		IRON	2%

*Contains less than 2% of the U.S. RDA of this nutrient.

Luscious raspberry preserves peek through tender, golden oatmeal cookies to create an eye-catching, taste-tempting treat.

Peekaberry Boos

1 cup firmly packed brown sugar
¾ cup sugar
1 cup margarine or butter, softened
½ cup water
1 teaspoon almond extract
2 eggs
3 cups Pillsbury's BEST® All
    Purpose or Unbleached Flour
2 cups quick-cooking rolled oats
1 teaspoon baking soda
½ teaspoon salt
½ teaspoon cinnamon
⅔ cup raspberry preserves

Heat oven to 400°F. In large bowl, beat brown sugar, sugar and margarine until light and fluffy. Add water, almond extract and eggs; blend well. (Mixture will look curdled.) Lightly spoon flour into measuring cup; level off. Stir in flour, rolled oats, baking soda, salt and cinnamon; mix well. Drop by rounded teaspoonfuls 2 inches apart onto ungreased cookie sheets. With spoon, make imprint in center of each cookie. Fill each imprint with ½ teaspoon preserves. Drop scant teaspoon dough over preserves on each cookie. Bake at 400°F. for 6 to 9 minutes or until light golden brown. Immediately remove from cookie sheets. 4½ to 5 dozen cookies.

HIGH ALTITUDE—Above 3500 Feet: Decrease sugar to ½ cup. Bake as directed above.

NUTRITION INFORMATION PER SERVING

SERVING SIZE: 1 COOKIE		PERCENT U.S. RDA PER SERVING	
CALORIES	100	PROTEIN	2%
PROTEIN	1g	VITAMIN A	2%
CARBOHYDRATE	15g	VITAMIN C	*
FAT	3g	THIAMINE	4%
CHOLESTEROL	8mg	RIBOFLAVIN	2%
SODIUM	75mg	NIACIN	*
POTASSIUM	35mg	CALCIUM	*
		IRON	2%

*Contains less than 2% of the U.S. RDA of this nutrient.

These moist, cake-like cookies can be made with an egg substitute, if desired, for those individuals trying to reduce cholesterol intake.

Almond Cookie Cakes

1 cup sugar
1 cup margarine or butter, softened
2 eggs or 4 oz. (½ cup) frozen
    cholesterol-free egg product,
    thawed
½ cup plain yogurt
2 teaspoons almond extract
2½ cups Pillsbury's BEST® All
    Purpose or Unbleached Flour
½ teaspoon baking soda
½ teaspoon salt
¾ cup slivered almonds
    Powdered sugar

Heat oven to 350°F. In large bowl, beat sugar and margarine until light and fluffy. Add eggs, yogurt and almond extract; blend well. (Mixture will look curdled.) Lightly spoon flour into measuring cup; level off. Stir in flour, baking soda and salt; mix well. Stir in almonds. Drop by rounded teaspoonfuls 2 inches apart onto ungreased cookie sheets. Bake at 350°F. for 10 to 14 minutes or until edges are light golden brown. Immediately remove from cookie sheets. Cool. Sprinkle with powdered sugar. 5 dozen cookies.

HIGH ALTITUDE—Above 3500 Feet: Increase flour to 2¾ cups. Bake as directed above.

NUTRITION INFORMATION PER SERVING

SERVING SIZE: 1 COOKIE		PERCENT U.S. RDA PER SERVING	
CALORIES	70	PROTEIN	*
PROTEIN	1g	VITAMIN A	2%
CARBOHYDRATE	8g	VITAMIN C	*
FAT	4g	THIAMINE	2%
CHOLESTEROL	8mg	RIBOFLAVIN	2%
SODIUM	65mg	NIACIN	*
POTASSIUM	25mg	CALCIUM	*
		IRON	*

*Contains less than 2% of the U.S. RDA of this nutrient.

Pictured on previous page: Peekaberry Boos

For packin' or snackin', this cookie is a favorite.

Granola Cookies

1 cup firmly packed brown sugar
½ cup sugar
½ cup shortening
½ cup margarine or butter, softened
1 teaspoon vanilla
2 eggs
1 cup Pillsbury's BEST® All Purpose
  or Unbleached Flour
1 cup Pillsbury's BEST® Whole
  Wheat Flour
½ teaspoon baking powder
½ teaspoon baking soda
½ teaspoon salt
2 cups granola

Heat oven to 350°F. In large bowl, beat brown sugar, sugar, shortening and margarine until light and fluffy. Add vanilla and eggs; blend well. Lightly spoon flour into measuring cup; level off. Stir in all purpose flour, whole wheat flour, baking powder, baking soda and salt; mix well. Stir in granola. Drop by teaspoonfuls 2 inches apart onto ungreased cookie sheets. Bake at 350°F. for 10 to 15 minutes or until edges are light golden brown. Cool 1 minute; remove from cookie sheets. 6 dozen cookies.

HIGH ALTITUDE—Above 3500 Feet: No change.

NUTRITION INFORMATION PER SERVING
SERVING SIZE:
1 COOKIE

		PERCENT U.S. RDA PER SERVING	
CALORIES	80	PROTEIN	*
PROTEIN	1g	VITAMIN A	*
CARBOHYDRATE	9g	VITAMIN C	*
FAT	4g	THIAMINE	2%
CHOLESTEROL	8mg	RIBOFLAVIN	*
SODIUM	45mg	NIACIN	*
POTASSIUM	40mg	CALCIUM	*
		IRON	2%

*Contains less than 2% of the U.S. RDA of this nutrient.

Macaroons, traditionally made with egg whites, team up with dates and high fiber oat bran for a delicious low fat, low cholesterol, sweet treat.

Chewy Date Bran Macaroons

2 egg whites
⅛ teaspoon salt
1 teaspoon vanilla
1 cup firmly packed brown sugar
1 cup chopped nuts
¾ cup oat bran
⅔ cup chopped dates

Heat oven to 350°F. Generously grease cookie sheets. In large bowl, beat egg whites, salt and vanilla until foamy. Gradually add brown sugar; beat until stiff peaks form, about 2 to 4 minutes. Fold in nuts, oat bran and dates. Drop by rounded teaspoonfuls 2 inches apart onto greased cookie sheets. Bake at 350°F. for 9 to 12 minutes or until lightly browned. Immediately remove from cookie sheets. 3 dozen cookies.

HIGH ALTITUDE—Above 3500 Feet: Decrease brown sugar to ⅔ cup. Bake as directed above.

NUTRITION INFORMATION PER SERVING
SERVING SIZE:
1 COOKIE

		PERCENT U.S. RDA PER SERVING	
CALORIES	60	PROTEIN	*
PROTEIN	1g	VITAMIN A	*
CARBOHYDRATE	10g	VITAMIN C	*
FAT	2g	THIAMINE	2%
CHOLESTEROL	0mg	RIBOFLAVIN	*
SODIUM	15mg	NIACIN	*
POTASSIUM	70mg	CALCIUM	*
		IRON	2%

*Contains less than 2% of the U.S. RDA of this nutrient.

  POPPIN' FRESH® HOMEMADE COOKIES

A BAKER'S DOZEN
OF ALL-TIME FAVORITES

A BAKER'S DOZEN
OF ALL-TIME FAVORITES

A potpourri
of the thirteen most popular cookies in America...

If you were shipwrecked on a desert island, what kind of cookies would you dream of — **Peanut Butter, Chocolate Chip, Oatmeal Raisin, Snickerdoodles, Ginger Snaps**? Or would it be **Peanut Blossoms** with their chocolate center or tender, buttery **Swedish Tea Cakes** (that also answer to Mexican Wedding Cakes, Russian Tea Cakes and Butterballs?) Or would visions of **All-Time Favorite Lemon Bars, Date Bars** or **Rolled Sugar Cookies** dance through your head? Probably any or all of them.

These are the cookies that have woven themselves into the tapestry of American life, the cookies that grandmothers offer from always-full cookie jars, that fill the house with tantalizing scents on chilly November days, that top off a box lunch at school or on the job, that win blue ribbons at the county fair.

This section offers a baker's dozen of these cookies, thirteen recipes that will conjure up memories of childhood and the cookies that became our favorites then and remain so today.

But of these all-time favorites, one would be chosen by far more than any other — Chocolate Chip Cookies. Like Brownies, they're an American phenomenon. Although we bake nearly 6 billion of them a year, Chocolate Chip Cookies have never caught on in other countries. Those 6 billion cookies are studded with more than 90 million bags of

chips. And for more than 50 years, they've been the cookie of first choice for millions of kids, teens, moms, dads, and grandparents.

Chocolate Chip Cookies were developed by chance in the 1930s. Like most cooks, Ruth Wakefield enjoyed toying with recipes. At her Toll House Inn in Whitman, Mass., she cut up a bar of semi-sweet chocolate and added the pieces to butter cookie dough. Instead of melting, the chocolate chunks softened into pockets of semi-sweet delight. And so an American tradition was born.

In this section you'll find two variations of the **Chocolate Chip Cookie** — **Chocolate Chunk Cookies** and **Kid-Sized Cookies**. The Chocolate Chunk calls for coarsely chopped chocolate in place of chips. Sheer delight for chocolate lovers. **Kid-Sized Cookies** substitute candy-coated chocolate pieces for chips, and sunflower seeds for chopped nuts. But the real surprise is their size: they're inches across and big enough to satisfy any kid's snack attack.

Another cookie recipe with a history is the one for **Peanut Blossoms**, which made its debut in 1957 as a prize winner in the Pillsbury Bake-Off® Contest. These cookies have been winners ever since, combining the creamy crunchiness of peanut butter cookies with rich sweet chocolate.

Pictured on previous page: Date Bars and Pinwheel Date Cookies p. 28

A delectable date filling is sandwiched between two irresistible crumb layers. These good old-fashioned bars are sure to inspire childhood memories of special church suppers or treats at grandma's house.

Date Bars

¼ cup firmly packed brown sugar
8-oz. pkg. (1½ cups) pitted dates, halved
½ cup water
½ teaspoon vanilla
1½ cups Pillsbury's BEST® All Purpose or Unbleached Flour
1 cup rolled oats
1 cup firmly packed brown sugar
½ cup chopped nuts
¼ teaspoon salt
¾ cup margarine or butter

Grease 13x9-inch pan. In medium saucepan, combine ¼ cup brown sugar, dates and water. Bring to a boil. Reduce heat; simmer 5 minutes or until thick. Remove from heat. Stir in vanilla. Cool.

Heat oven to 350°F. Lightly spoon flour into measuring cup; level off. In large bowl, combine flour, rolled oats, 1 cup brown sugar, nuts and salt. Using pastry blender or fork, cut in margarine until mixture resembles coarse crumbs. Reserve 2 cups of crumb mixture for topping. Press remaining crumb mixture firmly in bottom of greased pan. Spread evenly with date mixture. Sprinkle with reserved crumb mixture; pat lightly. Bake at 350°F. for 23 to 35 minutes or until golden brown. Cool completely. Cut into bars. 36 bars.

Every mouth-watering bite of these crispy-chewy oatmeal cookies is full of good-tasting nuts and raisins.

Oatmeal Raisin Cookies

¾ cup sugar
¼ cup firmly packed brown sugar
½ cup margarine or butter, softened
½ teaspoon vanilla
1 egg
¾ cup Pillsbury's BEST® All Purpose or Unbleached Flour
½ teaspoon baking soda
½ teaspoon cinnamon
¼ teaspoon salt
1½ cups quick-cooking rolled oats
½ cup raisins
½ cup chopped nuts

Heat oven to 375°F. Grease cookie sheets. In large bowl, beat sugar, brown sugar and margarine until light and fluffy. Add vanilla and egg; blend well. Lightly spoon flour into measuring cup; level off. Stir in flour, baking soda, cinnamon and salt; mix well. Stir in rolled oats, raisins and nuts. Drop by rounded teaspoonfuls 2 inches apart onto greased cookie sheets. Bake at 375°F. for 7 to 10 minutes or until edges are light golden brown. Cool 1 minute; remove from cookie sheets. 3½ dozen cookies.

HIGH ALTITUDE—Above 3500 Feet: Increase flour to 1 cup. Bake as directed above.

NUTRITION INFORMATION PER SERVING
SERVING SIZE:
1 BAR

		PERCENT U.S. RDA PER SERVING	
CALORIES	120	PROTEIN	2%
PROTEIN	1g	VITAMIN A	2%
CARBOHYDRATE	18g	VITAMIN C	*
FAT	5g	THIAMINE	4%
CHOLESTEROL	0mg	RIBOFLAVIN	2%
SODIUM	60mg	NIACIN	2%
POTASSIUM	90mg	CALCIUM	*
		IRON	4%

*Contains less than 2% of the U.S. RDA of this nutrient.

NUTRITION INFORMATION PER SERVING
SERVING SIZE:
1 COOKIE

		PERCENT U.S. RDA PER SERVING	
CALORIES	70	PROTEIN	*
PROTEIN	1g	VITAMIN A	2%
CARBOHYDRATE	10g	VITAMIN C	*
FAT	3g	THIAMINE	2%
CHOLESTEROL	6mg	RIBOFLAVIN	*
SODIUM	55mg	NIACIN	*
POTASSIUM	40mg	CALCIUM	*
		IRON	2%

*Contains less than 2% of the U.S. RDA of this nutrient.

These mouth-watering cookies with a marvelous date filling have long been favorites of all the "kids" who raid cookie jars.

Pinwheel Date Cookies

FILLING
- ¾ cup finely chopped dates
- ¼ cup sugar
- ⅓ cup water
- 2 tablespoons finely chopped nuts

COOKIES
- 1 cup firmly packed brown sugar
- ½ cup margarine or butter, softened
- 1 egg
- 1½ cups Pillsbury's BEST® All Purpose or Unbleached Flour
- 1½ teaspoons baking powder
- ¼ teaspoon salt

In small saucepan, combine dates, sugar and water. Bring to a boil. Reduce heat; cover and simmer 5 minutes or until thick. Stir in nuts. Cool.

In large bowl, beat brown sugar, margarine and egg until light and fluffy. Lightly spoon flour into measuring cup; level off. Stir in flour, baking powder and salt; mix at low speed until dough forms. Cover with plastic wrap; refrigerate 1 hour if necessary for easier handling.

On lightly floured surface, roll dough into 16x8-inch rectangle; carefully spread with date filling. Roll up, jelly-roll fashion, starting with 16-inch side; cut in half to form 2 shorter rolls. Cover; refrigerate at least 2 hours.

Heat oven to 375°F. Cut dough into ¼-inch slices. Place 2 inches apart on ungreased cookie sheets. Bake at 375°F. for 6 to 9 minutes or until light golden brown. Immediately remove from cookie sheets. 4½ to 5 dozen cookies.

HIGH ALTITUDE—Above 3500 Feet: Increase flour to 1½ cups plus 2 tablespoons. Bake as directed above.

Deliciously chewy macaroons are a snap to prepare and so inviting to serve with a cup of coffee.

Coconut Macaroons

- 2 egg whites
- ⅓ cup sugar
- 2 tablespoons flour
  Dash salt
- ¼ teaspoon almond extract
- 2 cups coconut

Heat oven to 325°F. Grease and lightly flour cookie sheet. In medium bowl, beat egg whites lightly. Add sugar, flour, salt and almond extract; blend well. Stir in coconut. Drop dough by tablespoonfuls 2 inches apart onto greased and floured cookie sheet. Bake at 325°F. for 13 to 17 minutes or until set and lightly browned. Immediately remove from cookie sheet. 12 cookies.

HIGH ALTITUDE—Above 3500 Feet: No change.

These simple cookies are so versatile. They combine well on a tray with other cookies; they can be cut into shapes to fit any occasion; they can be sprinkled with sugar, decorated or simply cut with a round scalloped cutter.

Rolled Sugar Cookies

  1 cup sugar
  1 cup margarine or butter, softened
  3 tablespoons milk
  1 teaspoon vanilla
  1 egg
  3 cups Pillsbury's BEST® All
      Purpose or Unbleached Flour
1½ teaspoons baking powder
  ½ teaspoon salt
    Sugar, if desired

In large bowl, combine 1 cup sugar, margarine, milk, vanilla and egg; blend well. Lightly spoon flour into measuring cup; level off. Stir in flour, baking powder and salt; mix well. Cover with plastic wrap; refrigerate 1 hour for easier handling.

Heat oven to 400°F. On lightly floured surface, roll dough, ⅓ at a time, to ⅛-inch thickness. Cut with floured cookie cutter. Place 1 inch apart on ungreased cookie sheets; sprinkle with sugar. Bake at 400°F. for 5 to 9 minutes or until edges are light brown. Immediately remove from cookie sheets. 5 to 6 dozen cookies.

HIGH ALTITUDE—Above 3500 Feet: Increase flour to 3 cups plus 2 tablespoons. Bake as directed above.

NUTRITION INFORMATION PER SERVING

SERVING SIZE: 1 COOKIE		PERCENT U.S. RDA PER SERVING	
CALORIES	60	PROTEIN	*
PROTEIN	1g	VITAMIN A	2%
CARBOHYDRATE	7g	VITAMIN C	*
FAT	3g	THIAMINE	2%
CHOLESTEROL	4mg	RIBOFLAVIN	*
SODIUM	50mg	NIACIN	*
POTASSIUM	10mg	CALCIUM	*
		IRON	*

*Contains less than 2% of the U.S. RDA of this nutrient.

In the nineteenth century "snickerdoodle" was a nonsense word used to describe any quickly made confection. Not only are these cookies quick to make but they are made with everyday ingredients that you probably have on hand.

Snickerdoodles

1½ cups sugar
  ½ cup margarine or butter, softened
  1 teaspoon vanilla
  2 eggs
2¾ cups Pillsbury's BEST® All
      Purpose or Unbleached Flour
  1 teaspoon cream of tartar
  ½ teaspoon baking soda
  ¼ teaspoon salt
  2 tablespoons sugar
  2 teaspoons cinnamon

Heat oven to 400°F. In large bowl, beat 1½ cups sugar and margarine until light and fluffy. Add vanilla and eggs; blend well. Lightly spoon flour into measuring cup; level off. Stir in flour, cream of tartar, baking soda and salt; mix well. In small bowl, combine 2 tablespoons sugar and cinnamon. Shape dough into 1-inch balls; roll in sugar-cinnamon mixture. Place 2 inches apart on ungreased cookie sheets. Bake at 400°F. for 8 to 10 minutes or until set. Immediately remove from cookie sheets. 4 dozen cookies.

HIGH ALTITUDE—Above 3500 Feet: No change.

NUTRITION INFORMATION PER SERVING

SERVING SIZE: 1 COOKIE		PERCENT U.S. RDA PER SERVING	
CALORIES	70	PROTEIN	*
PROTEIN	1g	VITAMIN A	*
CARBOHYDRATE	12g	VITAMIN C	*
FAT	2g	THIAMINE	2%
CHOLESTEROL	10mg	RIBOFLAVIN	2%
SODIUM	50mg	NIACIN	*
POTASSIUM	10mg	CALCIUM	*
		IRON	2%

*Contains less than 2% of the U.S. RDA of this nutrient.

POPPIN' FRESH® HOMEMADE COOKIES

Through the years, the classic chocolate chip cookie, with its many taste-tempting variations, has remained America's most popular cookie.

Chocolate Chip Cookies

¾ cup firmly packed brown sugar
½ cup sugar
½ cup margarine or butter, softened
½ cup shortening
1½ teaspoons vanilla
1 egg
1¾ cups Pillsbury's BEST® All Purpose or Unbleached Flour
1 teaspoon baking soda
½ teaspoon salt
6-oz. pkg. (1 cup) semi-sweet chocolate chips
½ cup chopped nuts or shelled sunflower seeds, if desired

Heat oven to 375°F. In large bowl, beat brown sugar, sugar, margarine and shortening until light and fluffy. Add vanilla and egg; blend well. Lightly spoon flour into measuring cup; level off. Stir in flour, baking soda and salt; mix well. Stir in chocolate chips and nuts. Drop by teaspoonfuls 2 inches apart onto ungreased cookie sheets. Bake at 375°F. for 8 to 10 minutes or until light golden brown. Cool 1 minute; remove from cookie sheets. 4 dozen cookies.

Chocolate Chunk Cookies: Substitute 8 oz. coarsely chopped semi-sweet chocolate for chocolate chips. Drop dough by tablespoonfuls 3 inches apart onto ungreased cookie sheets. Bake at 375°F. for 9 to 12 minutes or until light golden brown. Immediately remove from cookie sheets. 3 dozen cookies.

Kid-Sized Cookies: Prepare dough as directed in recipe omitting ½ cup sugar, 1 cup semi-sweet chocolate chips and ½ cup chopped nuts. Increase vanilla to 2 teaspoons. Stir 1 cup candy-coated chocolate pieces and ½ cup shelled sunflower seeds into prepared dough. Cover with plastic wrap; refrigerate if necessary for easier handling. Shape into 2-inch balls. Place 4 inches apart on ungreased cookie sheets. Press an additional ½ cup candy-coated chocolate pieces into balls to decorate tops of cookies. Bake at 350°F. for 15 to 20 minutes or until light golden brown. Cool 2 minutes; remove from cookie sheets. 14 large cookies.

HIGH ALTITUDE—Above 3500 Feet: No change.

NUTRITION INFORMATION PER SERVING
SERVING SIZE:
1 COOKIE

	PERCENT U.S. RDA PER SERVING
CALORIES 100	PROTEIN . . . .°
PROTEIN 1g	VITAMIN A . . . .°
CARBOHYDRATE 11g	VITAMIN C . . . .°
FAT 6g	THIAMINE 2%
CHOLESTEROL 6mg	RIBOFLAVIN . . . .°
SODIUM 70mg	NIACIN . . . .°
POTASSIUM 35mg	CALCIUM . . . .°
	IRON 2%

°Contains less than 2% of the U.S. RDA of this nutrient.

Kid-Sized Cookies

Easily prepared and always a familiar favorite with the traditional forked pattern, peanut butter cookies are a great bake sale cookie.

Peanut Butter Cookies

½ cup sugar
½ cup firmly packed brown sugar
½ cup margarine or butter, softened
½ cup peanut butter
2 tablespoons milk
1 teaspoon vanilla
1 egg
1¾ cups Pillsbury's BEST® All
    Purpose or Unbleached Flour
1 teaspoon baking soda
½ teaspoon salt
    Sugar

Heat oven to 375°F. In large bowl, beat sugar, brown sugar and margarine until light and fluffy. Add peanut butter, milk, vanilla and egg; blend well. Lightly spoon flour into measuring cup; level off. Stir in flour, baking soda and salt; mix well. Shape dough into 1-inch balls. Place 2 inches apart on ungreased cookie sheets. Flatten in crisscross pattern with fork dipped in sugar. Bake at 375°F. for 10 to 12 minutes or until golden brown. Immediately remove from cookie sheets. 3½ dozen cookies.

HIGH ALTITUDE—Above 3500 Feet: No change.

NUTRITION INFORMATION PER SERVING

SERVING SIZE: 1 COOKIE		PERCENT U.S. RDA PER SERVING	
CALORIES	80	PROTEIN	2%
PROTEIN	1g	VITAMIN A	*
CARBOHYDRATE	10g	VITAMIN C	*
FAT	4g	THIAMINE	2%
CHOLESTEROL	6mg	RIBOFLAVIN	*
SODIUM	95mg	NIACIN	2%
POTASSIUM	40mg	CALCIUM	*
		IRON	2%

*Contains less than 2% of the U.S. RDA of this nutrient.

Have you ever wondered where old-fashioned cookie favorites such as these originated? This cookie made its first appearance as a prize winner in Pillsbury's Bake-Off® contest in 1957.

Peanut Blossoms

1¾ cups Pillsbury's BEST® All
    Purpose or Unbleached Flour
½ cup sugar
½ cup firmly packed brown sugar
1 teaspoon baking soda
½ teaspoon salt
½ cup shortening
½ cup peanut butter
2 tablespoons milk
1 teaspoon vanilla
1 egg
    Sugar
    About 48 milk chocolate
    candy kisses

Heat oven to 375°F. Lightly spoon flour into measuring cup; level off. In large bowl, combine flour, ½ cup sugar, brown sugar, baking soda, salt, shortening, peanut butter, milk, vanilla and egg at low speed until stiff dough forms. Shape into 1-inch balls; roll in sugar. Place 2 inches apart on ungreased cookie sheets. Bake at 375°F. for 10 to 12 minutes or until golden brown. Immediately top each cookie with a candy kiss, pressing down firmly so cookie cracks around edge; remove from cookie sheets. 4 dozen cookies.

HIGH ALTITUDE—Above 3500 Feet: No change.

NUTRITION INFORMATION PER SERVING

SERVING SIZE: 1 COOKIE		PERCENT U.S. RDA PER SERVING	
CALORIES	100	PROTEIN	2%
PROTEIN	2g	VITAMIN A	*
CARBOHYDRATE	12g	VITAMIN C	*
FAT	5g	THIAMINE	2%
CHOLESTEROL	6mg	RIBOFLAVIN	2%
SODIUM	65mg	NIACIN	2%
POTASSIUM	55mg	CALCIUM	*
		IRON	2%

*Contains less than 2% of the U.S. RDA of this nutrient.

Peanut Blossoms

Enjoy the wonderful aroma of dark and fragrant gingerbread as you bake these flavorful ginger cookies.

Ginger Snaps

1 cup sugar
¾ cup margarine or butter, softened
¼ cup molasses
1 egg
2¼ cups Pillsbury's BEST® All Purpose or Unbleached Flour
2 teaspoons baking soda
1 teaspoon cinnamon
½ teaspoon salt
½ teaspoon ginger
½ teaspoon cloves
¼ teaspoon nutmeg
Sugar

In large bowl, beat 1 cup sugar, margarine, molasses and egg until light and fluffy. Lightly spoon flour into measuring cup; level off. Stir in flour, baking soda, cinnamon, salt, ginger, cloves and nutmeg; mix well. Cover with plastic wrap; refrigerate 1 hour for easier handling.

Heat oven to 350°F. Shape dough into 1-inch balls; roll in sugar. Place 2 inches apart on ungreased cookie sheets. Bake at 350°F. for 8 to 12 minutes or until set. (Cookies will puff up and flatten during baking.) Cool 1 minute; remove from cookie sheets. 4½ to 5 dozen cookies.

HIGH ALTITUDE — Above 3500 Feet: Decrease baking soda to 1½ teaspoons. Bake as directed above.

NUTRITION INFORMATION PER SERVING
SERVING SIZE: 1 COOKIE

		PERCENT U.S. RDA PER SERVING	
CALORIES	60	PROTEIN	*
PROTEIN	1g	VITAMIN A	*
CARBOHYDRATE	8g	VITAMIN C	*
FAT	2g	THIAMINE	2%
CHOLESTEROL	4mg	RIBOFLAVIN	*
SODIUM	85mg	NIACIN	*
POTASSIUM	20mg	CALCIUM	*
		IRON	*

*Contains less than 2% of the U.S. RDA of this nutrient.

These home-baked lemon bars, with a delicate crumb crust and mouth-watering lemon filling, have been a traditional favorite for generations of family gatherings and potlucks.

All-Time Favorite Lemon Bars

CRUST
1 cup Pillsbury's BEST® All Purpose or Unbleached Flour
¼ cup powdered sugar
½ cup margarine or butter

FILLING
2 eggs
1 cup sugar
2 tablespoons flour
2 to 3 teaspoons grated lemon peel
½ teaspoon baking powder
2 tablespoons lemon juice

Powdered sugar, if desired

Heat oven to 350°F. Lightly spoon flour into measuring cup; level off. In large bowl, combine 1 cup flour and powdered sugar. Using pastry blender or fork, cut in margarine until mixture resembles coarse crumbs. Press crumb mixture in bottom of ungreased 8 or 9-inch square pan. Bake at 350°F. for 15 minutes.

In small bowl, combine eggs and sugar; blend well. Stir in remaining filling ingredients. Pour filling over partially baked crust. Return to oven and bake for an additional 18 to 25 minutes or until light golden brown. Cool completely. Sprinkle with powdered sugar. Cut into bars. 24 bars.

HIGH ALTITUDE — Above 3500 Feet: No change.

NUTRITION INFORMATION PER SERVING
SERVING SIZE: 1 BAR

		PERCENT U.S. RDA PER SERVING	
CALORIES	100	PROTEIN	*
PROTEIN	1g	VITAMIN A	2%
CARBOHYDRATE	14g	VITAMIN C	*
FAT	4g	THIAMINE	2%
CHOLESTEROL	25mg	RIBOFLAVIN	2%
SODIUM	55mg	NIACIN	*
POTASSIUM	15mg	CALCIUM	*
		IRON	*

*Contains less than 2% of the U.S. RDA of this nutrient.

*Deliciously spiced and topped with cream
cheese frosting, these bars taste great
with a mug of hot apple cider.*

Pumpkin Bars

BARS
2 cups Pillsbury's BEST® All
    Purpose or Unbleached Flour
2 cups sugar
2 teaspoons baking powder
1 teaspoon baking soda
1 teaspoon cinnamon
1 teaspoon nutmeg
½ teaspoon salt
½ teaspoon cloves
1 cup oil
16-oz. can (2 cups) pumpkin
4 eggs

FROSTING
2 cups powdered sugar
⅓ cup margarine or butter,
    softened
3-oz. pkg. cream cheese, softened
1 tablespoon milk
1 teaspoon vanilla

Heat oven to 350°F. Grease
15x10x1-inch jelly roll pan. Lightly
spoon flour into measuring cup; level
off. In large bowl, blend all bar ingredients at low speed until moistened. Beat
2 minutes at medium speed. Pour into
greased pan. Bake at 350°F. for 25 to
30 minutes or until toothpick inserted
in center comes out clean. Cool
completely.

In small bowl, combine all frosting
ingredients; beat until smooth. Spread
over cooled bars. Store in refrigerator.
48 bars.

HIGH ALTITUDE—Above 3500 Feet:
Decrease baking soda to ½ teaspoon.
Bake at 375°F. for 30 to 35 minutes.

*This popular cookie is known by many
names: Butterballs, Mexican Wedding
Cakes and Russian Tea Cakes. Shapes
may vary from crescents to logs or balls
as in this recipe. These nutty butter cookies
are a perfect choice for holidays, gradua-
tions or any other special occasions.*

Swedish Tea Cakes

½ cup powdered sugar
1 cup margarine or butter, softened
2 teaspoons vanilla
2 cups Pillsbury's BEST® All
    Purpose or Unbleached Flour
1 cup finely chopped or ground
    almonds or pecans
¼ teaspoon salt
    Powdered sugar

Heat oven to 325°F. In large bowl,
beat ½ cup powdered sugar, margarine
and vanilla until light and fluffy. Lightly
spoon flour into measuring cup; level
off. Stir in flour, almonds and salt; mix
until dough forms. Shape into 1-inch
balls. Place 1 inch apart on ungreased
cookie sheets. Bake at 325°F. for 15 to
20 minutes or until set but not brown.
Immediately remove from cookie sheets.
Cool slightly; roll in powdered sugar.
Cool completely. Reroll in powdered
sugar. 5 dozen cookies.

HIGH ALTITUDE—Above 3500 Feet:
No change.

cookies for kids

To make with enjoyment or eat with delight...

When your herd of kids starts to wail, "Mom, there's nothing to do!", round them up and corral them in the kitchen for an afternoon of cookie baking. Not only will it solve the "nothing-to-do" dilemma, but it's fun and kids will learn a thing or two about weights and measures while they're at it. The cookies in this chapter were developed specifically with kids in mind to make with directions that are simple and easy to understand or to enjoy eating with sheer delight. Also, they make ample use of a microwave oven and limited equipment for easy clean up.

With refrigerated sugar cookie dough, frosting and red string licorice, kids can create **Cookie Balloons**. In less than five minutes, they can whip up a batch of **Granola Bark** in the microwave. It's a great after-school snack and activity. **Quick Chocolate Peanut Butter Cookie Pops** combine two ever-popular flavors in a no-bake cookie treat that's fun to eat.

For parties, let children enjoy **Windmills-On-A-Stick** or, make **Choose-A-Topping Cookie Pizza** or **Quick Chocolate Peanut Butter Cookie Pops**. The windmills resemble hand-held namesakes that kids find such fun on breezy days. Chocolate chips, raisins, candy-coated chocolate pieces and peanuts replace familiar pizza toppings on the cookie pizza. It's easy to prepare and ready to eat in about half an hour.

But before you turn kids loose in the kitchen, here are some tips to make the experience both safe and enjoyable.

Encourage them to:
- Wash their hands before handling food.
- Get all equipment out before beginning to cook.
- Read through the ingredient list and directions at least once before beginning the recipe.
- Ask for help or advice before they get started.

While they're cooking, teach them to:
- Use hot pads when handling hot cookie sheets and pans.
- Use knives safely by using a cutting board and cutting away from themselves.
- Wipe up floor spills to prevent falls.
- Turn handles of saucepans toward the center of the stove.

And once the baking's done, remind them that good cooks clean up after themselves and that includes:
- Doing all dishes and wiping off counter tops and tables.
- Turning off the oven.
- Returning ingredients and equipment to their original places.

Pictured on previous page: Windmills on a Stick

These fun cookies are sure to be a hit at a child's party. Because there is no sugar in the dough, there will be very little browning during baking. The delicately-sweet flavor comes from the sprinkled sugar topping.

Windmills on a Stick

¾ cup margarine or butter,
    softened
8-oz. pkg. cream cheese, softened
  1 egg, separated
  2 cups Pillsbury's BEST® All
    Purpose or Unbleached Flour
  1 tablespoon baking powder
 30 wooden sticks
 ⅔ cup colored sugar
 30 candy-coated chocolate pieces

In large bowl, beat margarine, cream cheese and egg yolk until smooth. Lightly spoon flour into measuring cup; level off. Stir in flour and baking powder; mix until stiff dough forms. Cover with plastic wrap; refrigerate 1 hour for easier handling.

Heat oven to 350°F. Lightly beat egg white; set aside. On lightly floured surface, roll dough, ½ at a time, into 15x9-inch rectangle. With pizza cutter, pastry wheel or sharp knife, cut dough into 3-inch squares. Place 3 inches apart on ungreased cookie sheets. Brush with beaten egg white. Lightly press about 1½ inches of wooden stick into bottom (center) of each dough square. With scissors or sharp knife, cut diagonally through dough from each corner to within ½ inch of center of each square. Sprinkle about 1 teaspoon colored sugar over each square. Fold alternate points of square to center to form windmill, overlapping and pinching gently to seal in center. Press 1 chocolate piece in center of each windmill. Bake at 350°F. for 9 to 12 minutes or until set. Using spatula, immediately remove from cookie sheets. 2½ dozen cookies.

HIGH ALTITUDE—Above 3500 Feet: No change.

NUTRITION INFORMATION PER SERVING

SERVING SIZE: 1 COOKIE		PERCENT U.S. RDA PER SERVING	
CALORIES	130	PROTEIN	2%
PROTEIN	2g	VITAMIN A	6%
CARBOHYDRATE	12g	VITAMIN C	*
FAT	8g	THIAMINE	4%
CHOLESTEROL	15mg	RIBOFLAVIN	2%
SODIUM	110mg	NIACIN	2%
POTASSIUM	20mg	CALCIUM	2%
		IRON	2%

*Contains less than 2% of the U.S. RDA of this nutrient.

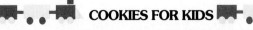

Children will love to create whimsical faces on the circles they cut out of Pillsbury All Ready Pie Crusts. The taste is reminiscent of those sweet treats Mom used to make with the leftover pie crust dough.

Funny Face Cookies

15-oz. pkg. Pillsbury All Ready
      Pie Crusts
  1 egg white
  1 teaspoon almond extract
    Sugar
    Sliced gumdrops, sliced
      jelly beans, chocolate
      chips or candy-coated
      chocolate pieces

Allow both crust pouches to stand at room temperature for 15 to 20 minutes. Heat oven to 450°F. In small bowl, lightly beat egg white and almond extract; set aside. Cut dough rounds from crusts with floured 2½-inch round cookie cutter (reserve dough scraps). Place 1 inch apart on ungreased cookie sheets. Brush with egg white mixture; sprinkle with sugar. Make funny faces with desired candy toppings and reserved dough scraps. Brush dough scraps with egg white mixture and sprinkle with sugar. Bake at 450°F. for 5 to 7 minutes or until light golden brown. Immediately remove from cookie sheets. 2 dozen cookies.

NUTRITION INFORMATION PER SERVING

SERVING SIZE: 1 COOKIE		PERCENT U.S. RDA PER SERVING	
CALORIES	100	PROTEIN	*
PROTEIN	1g	VITAMIN A	*
CARBOHYDRATE	11g	VITAMIN C	*
FAT	6g	THIAMINE	*
CHOLESTEROL	4mg	RIBOFLAVIN	*
SODIUM	110mg	NIACIN	*
POTASSIUM	10mg	CALCIUM	*
		IRON	*

*Contains less than 2% of the U.S. RDA of this nutrient.

Children have always been fascinated with balloons. These colorful balloon cookies with the long licorice strings are no exception. For variety make balloons of different colors.

Cookie Balloons

20-oz. pkg. Pillsbury's BEST®
      Refrigerated Sugar Cookies
      Colored sugar
      Pillsbury Frosting Supreme
      Ready To Spread
      Vanilla Frosting
  18 (10-inch) red string licorice

Heat oven to 350°F. Cut cookie dough into about thirty-six ¼-inch slices. Dip one cut side of each slice in colored sugar. Place sugar side up 2 inches apart on ungreased cookie sheets. Bake at 350°F. for 7 to 11 minutes or until golden brown. Cool slightly; remove from cookie sheets. Cool completely.

To make balloons, spread about 1 tablespoon frosting over bottom side of half of cookies. Press about 1 inch of end of licorice string into frosting on each cookie. Top each with second cookie. 18 sandwich cookies.

NUTRITION INFORMATION PER SERVING

SERVING SIZE: 1 SANDWICH COOKIE		PERCENT U.S. RDA PER SERVING	
CALORIES	280	PROTEIN	2%
PROTEIN	1g	VITAMIN A	*
CARBOHYDRATE	47g	VITAMIN C	*
FAT	10g	THIAMINE	4%
CHOLESTEROL	0mg	RIBOFLAVIN	6%
SODIUM	190mg	NIACIN	2%
POTASSIUM	25mg	CALCIUM	*
		IRON	2%

*Contains less than 2% of the U.S. RDA of this nutrient.

Funny Face Cookies

Most kids love to help make cookies. Even the youngest "bakers" can help mix and match the hearts in these lovable bear cutouts.

Big Heart Bears

CHOCOLATE PORTION

¼ **cup margarine or butter**
10 or 10.5-oz. **pkg. marshmallows**
2 oz. **(2 squares) semi-sweet chocolate, cut into pieces**
6 **cups crisp rice cereal**

PEPPERMINT PORTION

¼ **cup margarine or butter**
10 or 10.5-oz. **pkg. marshmallows**
2 to 3 **drops red food coloring**
½ **cup crushed peppermint candy**
6 **cups crisp rice cereal**

Line 15x10x1-inch jelly roll pan with foil. To prepare chocolate portion, melt margarine in large saucepan over medium heat. Add marshmallows and chocolate, stirring until smooth and completely melted. Remove from heat. Add cereal; stir until well coated. With wet fingers, press mixture evenly in foil-lined pan; refrigerate until firm. Remove from pan by lifting foil.

Line same 15x10x1-inch pan with foil. To prepare peppermint portion, melt margarine in large saucepan over medium heat. Add marshmallows and food coloring, stirring until smooth and completely melted. Remove from heat. Add peppermint candy and cereal; stir until well coated. With wet fingers, press mixture evenly in foil-lined pan; refrigerate until firm.

Using 5-inch bear-shaped or gingerbread man cookie cutter, cut shapes from each pan of cereal mixture. Using 1-inch heart-shaped canape cutter, cut hearts from center of each bear shape. Exchange hearts between bears so each bear will have opposite flavor heart. 16 bears.

■▮ MICROWAVE DIRECTIONS:
Line 15x10x1-inch jelly roll pan with foil. To prepare chocolate portion, place chocolate in 3-quart microwave-safe bowl. Microwave on HIGH for 1 minute. Add margarine and marshmallows; microwave on HIGH for 1 to 1½ minutes or until melted, stirring twice during cooking. Add cereal; stir until well coated. Continue as directed above for chocolate portion.

Line same 15x10x1-inch pan with foil. To prepare peppermint portion, place margarine in 3-quart microwave-safe bowl; microwave on HIGH for 45 to 60 seconds or until melted. Add marshmallows; toss to coat. Microwave on HIGH for 1 to 2 minutes or until marshmallows are puffed; stir until mixture is smooth. Add food coloring, peppermint candy and cereal; stir until well coated. Continue as directed above.

NUTRITION INFORMATION PER SERVING

SERVING SIZE: 1 BEAR		PERCENT U.S. RDA PER SERVING	
CALORIES	290	PROTEIN	2%
PROTEIN	2g	VITAMIN A	25%
CARBOHYDRATE	54g	VITAMIN C	10%
FAT	7g	THIAMINE	20%
CHOLESTEROL	0mg	RIBOFLAVIN	20%
SODIUM	330mg	NIACIN	20%
POTASSIUM	40mg	CALCIUM	*
		IRON	10%

*Contains less than 2% of the U.S. RDA of this nutrient.

Everyone will want to get into the act when you make these quick treats. It's so easy to dip store-bought cookies into your favorite flavor of candy coating.

Dip-a-Cookie Treats

8 oz. chocolate, vanilla or
   butterscotch-flavored
   candy coating

Any of the following cookies
   can be used:
   Creme-filled vanilla, chocolate
   or peanut butter sandwich
   cookies
   Vanilla wafers
   Shortbread cookies
   Sugar wafers
   Coconut bar cookies
   Fig bars
   Round buttery crackers filled
   with peanut butter

Melt candy coating in small saucepan over low heat, stirring constantly. Dip cookies halfway into coating; allow excess to drip off. Place on waxed paper until set. ¾ cup cookie coating.

■ MICROWAVE DIRECTIONS:
Place candy coating in small microwave-safe bowl. Microwave on HIGH for 1½ to 2 minutes, stirring once halfway through cooking. Stir until smooth. Continue as directed above.

NUTRITION INFORMATION: Variables in this recipe make it impossible to calculate nutrition information.

A rich chocolate shortbread is carefully scored and topped with vanilla milk chips before baking. As they come out of the oven, cut the cookies into intriguing little domino shapes. They will simply melt in your mouth.

Domino Cookies

1 cup powdered sugar
1 cup margarine or butter, softened
1 teaspoon vanilla
2 cups Pillsbury's BEST® All Purpose
   or Unbleached Flour
¼ cup unsweetened cocoa
   Vanilla milk chips

Heat oven to 325°F. In large bowl, beat powdered sugar and margarine until light and fluffy. Add vanilla; blend well. Lightly spoon flour into measuring cup; level off. Stir in flour and cocoa; mix well. Press dough out to form 12x6-inch rectangle on ungreased cookie sheet. With knife, score 5 lengthwise lines 1 inch apart and 11 crosswise lines 1 inch apart. Arrange vanilla milk chips flat side up inside score lines to resemble dots on dominoes. Bake at 325°F. for 20 to 23 minutes or until slightly firm to the touch. Immediately cut into 2x1-inch rectangles. Cool 5 minutes; remove from cookie sheet. 3 dozen cookies.

HIGH ALTITUDE— Above 3500 Feet: No change.

NUTRITION INFORMATION PER SERVING
SERVING SIZE:
1 COOKIE

	PERCENT U.S. RDA PER SERVING	
CALORIES 100	PROTEIN	*
PROTEIN 1g	VITAMIN A	4%
CARBOHYDRATE 10g	VITAMIN C	*
FAT 6g	THIAMINE	2%
CHOLESTEROL 0mg	RIBOFLAVIN	2%
SODIUM 65mg	NIACIN	*
POTASSIUM 20mg	CALCIUM	*
	IRON	2%

*Contains less than 2% of the U.S. RDA of this nutrient.

Fun-loving kids of all ages will enjoy making and eating these unbelievably easy, great-tasting cookie pops. Forever popular peanut butter is sandwiched between crisp vanilla wafers, then dipped in creamy chocolate.

Quick Chocolate Peanut Butter Cookie Pops

20 vanilla wafers
¼ cup peanut butter
10 wooden sticks
5 oz. chocolate-flavored
    candy coating

To assemble each cookie pop, spread about 1 teaspoon peanut butter over flat side of 1 vanilla wafer; press end of wooden stick into peanut butter. Top with plain vanilla wafer, placing flat sides together. Repeat for remaining cookie pops.

Melt candy coating in small saucepan over low heat, stirring constantly. Dip cookies into coating; allow excess to drip off.* Place on waxed paper until set. 10 cookie pops.

■ MICROWAVE DIRECTIONS: Assemble cookie pops as directed above. In 2-cup microwave-safe measuring cup, microwave candy coating on MEDIUM for 3 minutes or until melted, stirring once halfway through cooking. Stir until smooth. Continue as directed above.

TIP: *For easier dipping, pour melted candy coating into glass measuring cup or other tall narrow container.

NUTRITION INFORMATION PER SERVING

SERVING SIZE: 1 COOKIE POP	PERCENT U.S. RDA PER SERVING	
CALORIES 160	PROTEIN 4%	
PROTEIN 3g	VITAMIN A . . . . *	
CARBOHYDRATE 15g	VITAMIN C . . . . *	
FAT 10g	THIAMINE 10%	
CHOLESTEROL 2mg	RIBOFLAVIN 10%	
SODIUM 60mg	NIACIN 6%	
POTASSIUM 80mg	CALCIUM 2%	
	IRON . . . . *	

*Contains less than 2% of the U.S. RDA of this nutrient.

Quick Chocolate Peanut Butter Cookie Pops

Favorite sandwich spreads are now baked right into these luscious bars.

Peanut Butter and Jelly Bars

CRUST
1 cup Pillsbury's BEST® All Purpose
   or Unbleached Flour
½ cup rolled oats
½ cup firmly packed brown sugar
½ cup margarine or butter, chilled
¼ teaspoon salt
1 egg

FILLING
½ cup chopped peanuts
½ cup sugar
¾ cup peanut butter
1 egg white
½ cup jelly

Heat oven to 350°F. Lightly spoon flour into measuring cup; level off. In large bowl, combine all crust ingredients at low speed until crumbly. Reserve 1 cup of crumb mixture for topping.

Press remaining crumb mixture in bottom of ungreased 9-inch square pan. In same bowl, combine peanuts, sugar, peanut butter and egg white; beat well. Crumble and spread evenly over crust. Bake at 350°F. for 10 minutes. Spread jelly over peanut butter mixture; sprinkle with reserved crumb mixture. Return to oven and bake for an additional 25 to 30 minutes or until golden brown. Cool completely. Cut into bars. 24 bars.

HIGH ALTITUDE—Above 3500 Feet: No change.

NUTRITION INFORMATION PER SERVING

SERVING SIZE: 1 BAR		PERCENT U.S. RDA PER SERVING	
CALORIES	190	PROTEIN	6%
PROTEIN	4g	VITAMIN A	2%
CARBOHYDRATE	20g	VITAMIN C	*
FAT	10g	THIAMINE	4%
CHOLESTEROL	10mg	RIBOFLAVIN	2%
SODIUM	135mg	NIACIN	8%
POTASSIUM	115mg	CALCIUM	*
		IRON	4%

*Contains less than 2% of the U.S. RDA of this nutrient.

Be prepared for after-school munching. Keep a batch of these crunchy treats in the refrigerator.

Crispy Honey Drops

½ cup honey
¼ cup margarine or butter
3 cups cornflakes cereal
½ cup peanuts

Line cookie sheet with waxed paper. In large saucepan, combine honey and margarine. Bring to a boil; boil 2 minutes. Stir in cornflakes and peanuts until well coated. Drop by rounded tablespoonfuls onto waxed paper-lined cookie sheet.* Cool slightly; reshape if necessary. Refrigerate until set. Serve cold. Store in refrigerator. 24 cookies.

◼ MICROWAVE DIRECTIONS:
Line cookie sheet with waxed paper. In 2-quart microwave-safe bowl, combine honey and margarine. Microwave on HIGH for 1 to 1½ minutes or until margarine is melted; stir. Microwave on HIGH for 30 to 45 seconds or until mixture boils. Continue to microwave on HIGH for 2 minutes. Continue as directed above.

TIP: *If desired, mixture can be spooned into paper candy cups.

HIGH ALTITUDE—Above 3500 Feet: No change.

NUTRITION INFORMATION PER SERVING
SERVING SIZE:
1 COOKIE

	PERCENT U.S. RDA PER SERVING	
CALORIES............70	PROTEIN.............*	
PROTEIN.............1g	VITAMIN A.........4%	
CARBOHYDRATE.......9g	VITAMIN C.........2%	
FAT.................3g	THIAMINE..........2%	
CHOLESTEROL........0mg	RIBOFLAVIN........2%	
SODIUM.............75mg	NIACIN............4%	
POTASSIUM..........25mg	CALCIUM...........*	
	IRON..............*	

*Contains less than 2% of the U.S. RDA of this nutrient.

Enjoy four sensational toppings on one pizza-sized, quick-to-prepare cookie. It's sliced and served in wedges. The only hard part is choosing which flavor to try first.

Choose-a-Topping Cookie Pizza

20-oz. pkg. Pillsbury's BEST® Refrigerated Sugar Cookies

TOPPINGS
½ cup candy-coated chocolate pieces
½ cup chocolate, butterscotch or vanilla milk chips
½ cup raisins
½ cup peanuts or chocolate-covered peanuts

Heat oven to 350°F. Line 12-inch pizza pan with foil; grease foil. Press cookie dough into bottom of greased, foil-lined pan. Score dough into 4 equal wedges. Top each wedge with ½ cup of a topping. Bake at 350°F. for 20 to 28 minutes or until golden brown. Cool completely. Remove cookie and foil from pan; remove foil from cookie. Cut into wedges. 16 servings.

NUTRITION INFORMATION PER SERVING
SERVING SIZE:
1/16 OF RECIPE

	PERCENT U.S. RDA PER SERVING	
CALORIES..........260	PROTEIN...........4%	
PROTEIN.............3g	VITAMIN A.........*	
CARBOHYDRATE......34g	VITAMIN C.........*	
FAT................12g	THIAMINE..........6%	
CHOLESTEROL........0mg	RIBOFLAVIN........8%	
SODIUM.............190mg	NIACIN............6%	
POTASSIUM..........100mg	CALCIUM...........2%	
	IRON..............6%	

*Contains less than 2% of the U.S. RDA of this nutrient.

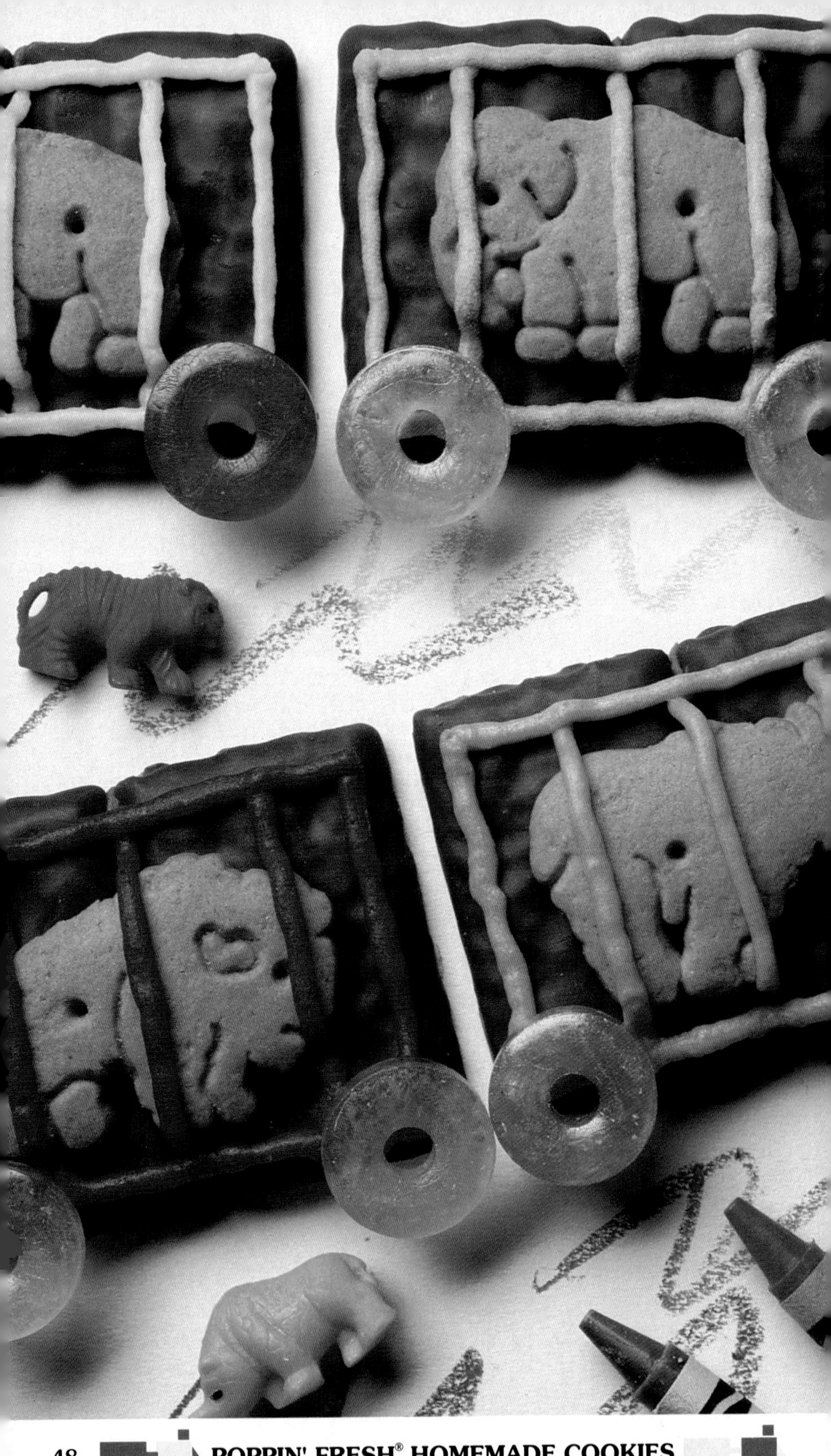

"I think I can, I think I can, I think I can..." We think this circus train full of animals is sure to make it to the top of your child's list of favorites.

Circus Cookie Train

22	(2 x 1½-inch) chocolate-covered graham crackers*
4.5-oz.	can Pillsbury Decorator Icing
11	animal crackers
2 (.90-oz.)	pkg. fruit flavored, ring-shaped hard candies

To assemble each cookie, pipe strip of frosting along outer edge of one 2-inch side of 1 graham cracker. Press 2-inch edge of second graham cracker into frosted edge to form 3x2-inch rectangle. Using writing tip, pipe frosting around outer edge of rectangle. Place 1 animal cracker lengthwise in center of rectangle. Pipe 3 vertical lines 1 inch apart over graham crackers and animal cracker to resemble cage. Attach 1 ring-shaped candy to lower left and 1 to lower right corner to resemble wheels on cage. Repeat with remaining graham crackers, animal crackers, icing and candies. Arrange cookies side by side on serving tray to form train. 11 cookies.

TIP: *Eleven larger chocolate-covered graham crackers can be substituted. Omit first step of frosting 2 graham crackers together.

NUTRITION INFORMATION PER SERVING

SERVING SIZE: 1 COOKIE		PERCENT U.S. RDA PER SERVING	
CALORIES	190	PROTEIN	2%
PROTEIN	2g	VITAMIN A	*
CARBOHYDRATE	29g	VITAMIN C	*
FAT	7g	THIAMINE	2%
CHOLESTEROL	0mg	RIBOFLAVIN	8%
SODIUM	120mg	NIACIN	2%
POTASSIUM	90mg	CALCIUM	2%
		IRON	6%

*Contains less than 2% of the U.S. RDA of this nutrient.

Circus Cookie Train

Melted butterscotch chips and marsh-mallows combine with ever-popular popcorn and peanuts for a real kid-pleasin' bar.

Popcorn Bars

10 cups popped popcorn
1 cup salted peanuts
10 or 10.5-oz. pkg. marshmallows
1 cup butterscotch
  chips*
⅓ cup margarine or
  butter

Lightly grease 13x9-inch pan. In large bowl, combine popcorn and peanuts. In large saucepan, melt marshmallows, butterscotch chips and margarine over low heat, stirring occasionally. Pour marshmallow mixture over popcorn-peanut mixture; stir until well coated. With buttered hands, press firmly in greased pan. Refrigerate until set. Cut into bars. 36 bars.

◨ MICROWAVE DIRECTIONS:
Lightly grease 13x9-inch pan. In large bowl, combine popcorn and peanuts. In large microwave-safe bowl, combine marshmallows and margarine. Micro-wave on HIGH for 2½ to 3 minutes, stirring after each minute. Stir until smooth. Add butterscotch chips. Micro-wave on HIGH for 30 to 45 seconds or until chips begin to melt. Stir until smooth. Continue as directed above.

TIP: *One 6-oz. pkg. (1 cup) semi-sweet chocolate chips or 1 cup peanut butter chips can be substituted.

NUTRITION INFORMATION PER SERVING

SERVING SIZE: 1 BAR		PERCENT U.S. RDA PER SERVING	
CALORIES	110	PROTEIN	2%
PROTEIN	2g	VITAMIN A	*
CARBOHYDRATE	14g	VITAMIN C	*
FAT	5g	THIAMINE	2%
CHOLESTEROL	0mg	RIBOFLAVIN	*
SODIUM	55mg	NIACIN	2%
POTASSIUM	40mg	CALCIUM	*
		IRON	*

*Contains less than 2% of the U.S. RDA of this nutrient.

When the kids come home from school and crave something sweet, they can make this irresistibly tempting bark in the microwave in less than five minutes.

Granola Bark

12 oz. vanilla-flavored candy
  coating
2 cups granola

Line cookie sheet with waxed paper. Melt candy coating in medium sauce-pan over low heat, stirring constantly. Stir in granola until well coated. Spread mixture on waxed paper-lined cookie sheet. Refrigerate until set. Break into serving-sized pieces. 19 ounces.

◨ MICROWAVE DIRECTIONS:
Line cookie sheet with waxed paper. In 1-quart microwave-safe bowl or 4-cup microwave-safe measuring cup, micro-wave candy coating on MEDIUM for 3 to 4 minutes or until melted, stirring once halfway through cooking. Stir until smooth. Continue as directed above.

NUTRITION INFORMATION PER SERVING

SERVING SIZE: 1 OUNCE		PERCENT U.S. RDA PER SERVING	
CALORIES	170	PROTEIN	2%
PROTEIN	2g	VITAMIN A	*
CARBOHYDRATE	17g	VITAMIN C	*
FAT	11g	THIAMINE	15%
CHOLESTEROL	0mg	RIBOFLAVIN	10%
SODIUM	15mg	NIACIN	2%
POTASSIUM	95mg	CALCIUM	2%
		IRON	2%

*Contains less than 2% of the U.S. RDA of this nutrient.

Even the tiniest hands can help Mom or Dad roll these peanut butter-coated marshmallows in the crisp cereal. Watch the pride on their faces when the cookie plate is passed.

Marshmallow Balls

5 to 6 cups crisp rice cereal or ready-sweetened chocolate-flavored rice cereal
1 cup peanut butter chips
¼ cup margarine or butter
14-oz. can sweetened condensed milk (not evaporated)
10-oz. pkg. (about 40) large marshmallows

Place cereal in shallow bowl. In small saucepan, melt peanut butter chips and margarine with condensed milk over low heat, stirring occasionally. Cool slightly. Using two forks, dip each marsh-mallow in peanut butter mixture; roll in cereal. Place on waxed paper until dry. 40 cookies.

▄▮ MICROWAVE DIRECTIONS:
In medium microwave-safe bowl, combine peanut butter chips, margarine and condensed milk. Microwave on HIGH for 1½ to 2 minutes or until peanut butter chips are melted, stirring once halfway through cooking. Stir until smooth. Continue as directed above.

NUTRITION INFORMATION PER SERVING

SERVING SIZE: 1 COOKIE		PERCENT U.S. RDA PER SERVING	
CALORIES	120	PROTEIN	2%
PROTEIN	2g	VITAMIN A	6%
CARBOHYDRATE	19g	VITAMIN C	2%
FAT	4g	THIAMINE	4%
CHOLESTEROL	4mg	RIBOFLAVIN	6%
SODIUM	95mg	NIACIN	6%
POTASSIUM	75mg	CALCIUM	4%
		IRON	2%

These eye-catching cookies are baked in a waffle iron and are especially delicious eaten warm.

Chocolate Tic Tac Doughs

⅓ cup firmly packed brown sugar
¼ cup margarine or butter, softened
1 tablespoon milk
1 teaspoon almond extract
1 egg
⅔ cup Pillsbury's BEST® All Purpose or Unbleached Flour
4 teaspoons unsweetened cocoa
½ teaspoon baking powder

Heat waffle iron to medium. In small bowl, combine brown sugar, margarine, milk, almond extract and egg; blend well. (Mixture will look curdled.) Lightly spoon flour into measuring cup; level off. Stir in flour, cocoa and baking powder; mix well. Drop by teaspoonfuls 1 inch apart onto hot waffle iron. Close lid and bake 1 minute or until firm. Immediately remove from waffle iron. 20 cookies.

HIGH ALTITUDE—Above 3500 Feet: No change.

NUTRITION INFORMATION PER SERVING

SERVING SIZE: 1 COOKIE		PERCENT U.S. RDA PER SERVING	
CALORIES	60	PROTEIN	*
PROTEIN	1g	VITAMIN A	2%
CARBOHYDRATE	7g	VITAMIN C	*
FAT	3g	THIAMINE	*
CHOLESTEROL	15mg	RIBOFLAVIN	*
SODIUM	40mg	NIACIN	*
POTASSIUM	25mg	CALCIUM	*
		IRON	2%

*Contains less than 2% of the U.S. RDA of this nutrient.

BARS – A PANFUL OF PLEASURE

The versatile, portable cookies for any occasion...

"I never met a bar I didn't like." Well, maybe that's not quite what Will Rogers said, but it's a statement that's hard to question. When someone says, "I'll bring bars," you know that dessert's well taken care of and that it will be delicious. That's the beauty of bars: whether elegant or hearty, they're a snap to make, they can be toted anywhere, and they're simply good to eat. In this selection of recipes, we guarantee you won't find a bar you don't like. There are bars for potlucks, bars for graduation parties, bars for gifts, bars for the holidays. There are bars with a healthful twist, bars that use mixes, bars from scratch and bars that aren't baked at all.

When you want your bars a bit more nutritious, choose **Bran Bars** made with bran cereal and raisins, or moist, flavorful **Zucchini Bars** that can also help you put a dent in your garden's overabundance of zucchini.

For bars that are more candy than cookie, give **Chocolate-Caramel Squares** a try. Melted caramels are layered between cream-filled sugar wafer cookies and then spread with semi-sweet chocolate. Another candy-like bar, **Coconut-Almond Bars**, are reminiscent of a popular candy bar.

In this chapter, you'll also find a special assortment of recipes for that Yankee Doodle Dandy of bars—brownies. When it comes to brownies, Americans know just what they like. According to a national survey, 58% of consumers prefer their brownies thin, somewhat moist and chewy. Thirty-two percent like theirs very moist and fudge-like. And if the brownies themselves weren't enough, most of us want something on top of our favorite kind: nuts, frosting or chocolate chips.

Brownies, like Chocolate Chip Cookies, are an American invention. No one knows who concocted the first batch, but recipes appeared as early as 1896 in *The Fannie Farmer Cookbook* and Sears and Roebuck printed one in their 1897 catalog. The first brownies were probably a surprising mistake: someone forgot to add baking powder to their chocolate cake batter. What at first appeared to be a sunken mess, turned out to be a tasty confection that captured a country's affections.

If you like your brownies rich, chocolatey and easy to make, start with the basic recipe in this section. It's stirred together in a saucepan. For brownies with a tropical twist, try **Aloha Brownies** with pineapple and coconut and spread with cream cheese frosting or **Banana Brownies** studded with chocolate chips and topped with mocha butter frosting.

Pictured on previous page: Grasshopper Brownies p. 56, Cappucino Fudge Brownies p. 57 and Banana Brownies with Mocha Frosting p. 56

These sensational brownies are stirred together very quickly in a saucepan. Serve them just as they are, or frost them with your favorite frosting, or sprinkle them with powdered sugar.

Brownies

½ cup margarine or butter
2 oz. (2 squares) unsweetened chocolate or 2 envelopes premelted unsweetened baking chocolate
1 cup sugar
1 teaspoon vanilla
2 eggs
⅔ cup Pillsbury's BEST® All Purpose or Unbleached Flour
½ cup chopped nuts, if desired
½ teaspoon baking powder
¼ teaspoon salt

Heat oven to 350°F. Grease and lightly flour bottom only of 8 or 9-inch square pan. In large saucepan, melt margarine and chocolate over low heat, stirring constantly. Remove from heat; cool slightly. Blend in sugar and vanilla. Beat in eggs, one at a time. Lightly spoon flour into measuring cup; level off. Stir in flour and remaining ingredients. Spread in greased and floured pan. Bake at 350°F. for 20 to 25 minutes or until set in center. Cool completely. Cut into bars. 24 bars.

HIGH ALTITUDE—Above 3500 Feet: Decrease baking powder to ¼ teaspoon. Bake as directed above.

NUTRITION INFORMATION PER SERVING
SERVING SIZE:
BAR

		PERCENT U.S. RDA PER SERVING	
CALORIES	120	PROTEIN	2%
PROTEIN	2g	VITAMIN A	2%
CARBOHYDRATE	12g	VITAMIN C	*
FAT	7g	THIAMINE	2%
CHOLESTEROL	25mg	RIBOFLAVIN	2%
SODIUM	80mg	NIACIN	*
POTASSIUM	45mg	CALCIUM	*
		IRON	2%

*Contains less than 2% of the U.S. RDA of this nutrient.

The outstanding flavor combination of peanut butter and chocolate is perfectly complemented by coconut in these rich, great-tasting brownies.

Peanut Butter Macaroon Brownies

BASE
2 cups sugar
1 cup margarine or butter, softened
1¼ teaspoons vanilla
4 eggs
1½ cups Pillsbury's BEST® All Purpose or Unbleached Flour
⅔ cup unsweetened cocoa
1 cup peanut butter chips

TOPPING
14-oz. can sweetened condensed milk (not evaporated)
7-oz. pkg. (2⅔ cups) coconut
6-oz. pkg. (1 cup) semi-sweet chocolate chips

Heat oven to 350°F. Grease 15x10x1-inch jelly roll pan. In large bowl, beat sugar, margarine and vanilla until light and fluffy. Add eggs, one at a time, beating well after each addition. Lightly spoon flour into measuring cup; level off. Add flour and cocoa; mix well. Stir in peanut butter chips. Spread in greased pan.

In small bowl, combine all topping ingredients. Spoon topping by tea-spoonfuls over base; spread carefully. Bake at 350°F. for 27 to 32 minutes or until topping is light golden brown. Cool completely. Cut into bars. 36 bars.

HIGH ALTITUDE—Above 3500 Feet: No change.

NUTRITION INFORMATION PER SERVING
SERVING SIZE:
1 BAR

		PERCENT U.S. RDA PER SERVING	
CALORIES	250	PROTEIN	6%
PROTEIN	4g	VITAMIN A	6%
CARBOHYDRATE	31g	VITAMIN C	*
FAT	12g	THIAMINE	4%
CHOLESTEROL	35mg	RIBOFLAVIN	6%
SODIUM	110mg	NIACIN	4%
POTASSIUM	140mg	CALCIUM	6%
		IRON	4%

*Contains less than 2% of the U.S. RDA of this nutrient.

This popular brownie with the fluffy mint frosting was originally made with refrigerated spread 'n bake brownies. This new version is made with brownie mix for that same rich, fudgy flavor.

Grasshopper Brownies

BROWNIES
21½-oz. pkg. Pillsbury Fudge
      Brownie Mix
  ½ cup water
  ½ cup oil
  1 egg

FILLING
  4 cups powdered sugar
3-oz. pkg. cream cheese, softened
  ¼ cup margarine or butter,
      softened
3 to 4 tablespoons milk
  1 teaspoon vanilla
  ¼ teaspoon peppermint extract
4 to 6 drops green food coloring

GLAZE
  1 oz. (1 square) unsweetened
      chocolate
  1 tablespoon margarine or
      butter

Heat oven to 350°F. Grease bottom only of 13x9-inch pan. Prepare and bake brownie mix according to package directions. Cool completely.

In large bowl, combine all filling ingredients; beat at medium speed until smooth. Spread over cooled brownies.

In small saucepan, melt chocolate and 1 tablespoon margarine over low heat, stirring occasionally; drizzle over filling. Refrigerate before cutting. Store in refrigerator. 36 bars.

HIGH ALTITUDE—Above 3500 Feet: Add ¼ cup flour to dry brownie mix. Bake as directed above.

The unbeatable flavors of banana, chocolate and mocha come together in this moist brownie.

Banana Brownies with Mocha Frosting

21½-oz. pkg. Pillsbury Fudge
      Brownie Mix
  ½ cup water
  ½ cup oil
  ½ cup (1 large) mashed banana
  1 egg
  ½ cup semi-sweet chocolate
      chips

FROSTING
  3 tablespoons unsweetened
      cocoa
  1 teaspoon instant coffee
      granules or crystals
  ⅓ cup margarine or butter,
      softened
  4 cups powdered sugar
  ¼ teaspoon salt
  1 teaspoon vanilla
5 to 6 tablespoons milk

Heat oven to 350°F. Grease bottom only of 13x9-inch pan. In large bowl, combine brownie mix, water, oil, banana and egg; beat 50 strokes by hand. Stir in chocolate chips. Spread in greased pan. Bake at 350°F. for 28 to 35 minutes. DO NOT OVERBAKE. Cool completely.

In large bowl, beat cocoa, coffee granules and margarine until light and fluffy. Add remaining frosting ingredients, adding enough milk until frosting is of desired spreading consistency; blend until smooth. Spread over cooled brownies. Cut into bars. 36 bars.

HIGH ALTITUDE—Above 3500 Feet: Add ⅓ cup flour to dry brownie mix; decrease oil to ⅓ cup. Bake at 350°F. for 30 to 40 minutes.

NUTRITION INFORMATION PER SERVING

SERVING SIZE: 1 BAR		PERCENT U.S. RDA PER SERVING	
CALORIES	170	PROTEIN	2%
PROTEIN	1g	VITAMIN A	*
CARBOHYDRATE	27g	VITAMIN C	*
FAT	7g	THIAMINE	2%
CHOLESTEROL	8mg	RIBOFLAVIN	2%
SODIUM	100mg	NIACIN	*
POTASSIUM	75mg	CALCIUM	*
		IRON	2%

*Contains less than 2% of the U.S. RDA of this nutrient.

Cappucino, a traditional beverage of Italy, is a coffee served with a foamy head of milk or cream. Superb coffee flavor permeates these elegant brownies of the same name.

Cappucino Fudge Brownies

BROWNIES
   5 oz. (5 squares) unsweetened chocolate, cut into pieces
   ¾ cup butter or margarine
   2 tablespoons instant coffee granules or crystals
   1 tablespoon vanilla
  2¼ cups sugar
   1 teaspoon cinnamon
   4 eggs
  1⅓ cups Pillsbury's BEST® All Purpose or Unbleached Flour
  1½ cups coarsely chopped pecans

FROSTING
   ½ cup butter or margarine, softened
   2 cups powdered sugar
   ½ teaspoon vanilla
   2 tablespoons brewed coffee

GLAZE
   1 oz. (1 square) semi-sweet chocolate
   1 teaspoon shortening

Heat oven to 375°F. Grease 13x9-inch pan. In small saucepan, melt unsweetened chocolate and ¾ cup butter over low heat, stirring occasionally. Remove from heat. Stir in coffee granules and 1 tablespoon vanilla; set aside.

In large bowl, beat sugar, cinnamon and eggs about 7 minutes or until sugar is dissolved. Lightly spoon flour into measuring cup; level off. Fold chocolate mixture, flour and pecans into egg mixture just until blended. Pour batter into greased pan. Bake at 375°F. for 25 to 35 minutes. DO NOT OVERBAKE. Cool completely.

In small bowl, beat ½ cup butter until light and fluffy. Add powdered sugar, ½ teaspoon vanilla and brewed coffee. Beat until smooth. Spread over cooled brownies.

In small saucepan, melt semi-sweet chocolate with shortening over low heat, stirring occasionally. Drizzle glaze in horizontal parallel lines about 1 inch apart over top of brownies. Immediately draw knife through glaze in straight vertical lines to form pattern. Refrigerate until firm. Cut into bars. 36 bars.

HIGH ALTITUDE—Above 3500 Feet: No change.

NUTRITION INFORMATION PER SERVING

SERVING SIZE: 1 BAR		PERCENT U.S. RDA PER SERVING	
CALORIES	220	PROTEIN	2%
PROTEIN	2g	VITAMIN A	6%
CARBOHYDRATE	24g	VITAMIN C	*
FAT	13g	THIAMINE	2%
CHOLESTEROL	50mg	RIBOFLAVIN	2%
SODIUM	75mg	NIACIN	*
POTASSIUM	70mg	CALCIUM	*
		IRON	4%

*Contains less than 2% of the U.S. RDA of this nutrient.

*These blondies (brownies without choc-
olate) are topped with a rich, buttery
frosting. Butter will enhance the wonderful
frosting flavor.*

Pecan Blondies with Browned Butter Frosting

BARS

1	cup sugar
½	cup firmly packed brown sugar
½	cup butter or margarine, softened
1	teaspoon vanilla
2	eggs
1½	cups Pillsbury's BEST® All Purpose or Unbleached Flour
1	teaspoon baking powder
½	teaspoon salt
½	cup chopped pecans

FROSTING

2	tablespoons butter or margarine
2	cups powdered sugar
¼	teaspoon vanilla
2 to 4	tablespoons milk

Pecan halves, if desired

Heat oven to 350°F. Grease 13x9-inch
pan. In large bowl, beat sugar, brown
sugar and ½ cup butter until light and
fluffy. Add 1 teaspoon vanilla and eggs;
blend well. Lightly spoon flour into
measuring cup; level off. Stir in flour,
baking powder and salt; mix well. Stir in
½ cup pecans. Spread in greased pan.
Bake at 350°F. for 23 to 33 minutes
or until toothpick inserted in center
comes out clean. Cool completely.

Heat 2 tablespoons butter in medium
saucepan over medium heat until light
golden brown. Remove from heat. Stir
in powdered sugar, ¼ teaspoon vanilla,
and enough milk for desired spreading
consistency; blend until smooth. Spread
over cooled bars. Arrange pecan halves
over frosting. Cut into bars. 36 bars.

Pecan Blondies with Browned Butter Frosting

HIGH ALTITUDE — Above 3500 Feet:
Increase flour to 1¾ cups. Decrease
sugar to ½ cup. Bake as directed above.

NUTRITION INFORMATION PER SERVING

SERVING SIZE: 1 BAR		PERCENT U.S. RDA PER SERVING	
CALORIES	120	PROTEIN	°
PROTEIN	1g	VITAMIN A	2%
CARBOHYDRATE	19g	VITAMIN C	°
FAT	5g	THIAMINE	2%
CHOLESTEROL	25mg	RIBOFLAVIN	2%
SODIUM	75mg	NIACIN	°
POTASSIUM	30mg	CALCIUM	°
		IRON	2%

*Contains less than 2% of the U.S. RDA of this nutrient.

*Hazelnuts transform this convenient
brownie mix into a gourmet treat.*

Hazelnut Brownies

21½-oz.	pkg. Pillsbury Fudge Brownie Mix
1	cup chopped hazelnuts (filberts), toasted*
½	cup water
½	cup oil
2	tablespoons hazelnut-flavored liqueur, if desired
1	egg

Heat oven to 350°F. Grease bottom
only of 13x9-inch pan. In large bowl,
combine all ingredients; beat 50 strokes
by hand. Spread in greased pan. Bake
at 350°F. for 30 to 35 minutes or until
set. DO NOT OVERBAKE. Cool completely. Cut into bars. 36 bars.

TIP: *To toast hazelnuts, spread on cookie
sheet; bake at 375°F. for 4 to 8 minutes or until golden brown, stirring
occasionally. Or, spread hazelnuts in
thin layer in microwave-safe pie pan.
Microwave on HIGH for 3½ to 4 minutes or until golden brown, stirring
frequently.

HIGH ALTITUDE — Above 3500 Feet:
Add ¼ cup flour to dry brownie mix.
Bake as directed above.

NUTRITION INFORMATION PER SERVING

SERVING SIZE: 1 BAR		PERCENT U.S. RDA PER SERVING	
CALORIES	120	PROTEIN	2%
PROTEIN	1g	VITAMIN A	°
CARBOHYDRATE	15g	VITAMIN C	°
FAT	6g	THIAMINE	2%
CHOLESTEROL	8mg	RIBOFLAVIN	°
SODIUM	60mg	NIACIN	°
POTASSIUM	60mg	CALCIUM	°
		IRON	°

*Contains less than 2% of the U.S. RDA of this nutrient.

The flavors of pineapple and coconut complement rich chocolate to bake into a unique taste of the tropics.

Aloha Brownies

BROWNIES
21¾-oz. pkg. Pillsbury Fudge Walnut
         Brownie Mix
   ½ cup oil
   1 egg
8-oz. can crushed pineapple in
         its own juice, drained
   ½ cup coconut

FROSTING
   2 cups powdered sugar
3-oz. pkg. cream cheese, softened
   ½ teaspoon vanilla
1 to 3 teaspoons milk

Heat oven to 350°F. Grease bottom only of 13x9-inch pan. In large bowl, combine all brownie ingredients; beat 50 strokes by hand or until well blended. Spread in greased pan. Bake at 350°F. for 30 to 35 minutes. DO NOT OVER-BAKE. Cool completely.

In small bowl, combine all frosting ingredients, adding enough milk until frosting is of desired spreading consistency; blend until smooth. Spread over cooled brownies. Cut into bars. Store in refrigerator. 24 bars.

HIGH ALTITUDE—Above 3500 Feet: Add ¼ cup flour to dry brownie mix. Bake as directed above.

Chocolate-Caramel Squares

These delightful no-bake bars are like a scrumptious candy bar. Gooey caramel filling is surrounded by layers of crisp wafer cookies and topped with rich, creamy chocolate. For an added touch, use cookie wafers of assorted colors.

Chocolate-Caramel Squares

8½ or 9-oz. pkg. cream-filled sugar
         wafer cookies
   24 vanilla caramels,
         unwrapped
   2 tablespoons milk
6-oz. pkg. (1 cup) semi-sweet
         chocolate chips
   3 tablespoons margarine
         or butter

NUTRITION INFORMATION PER SERVING

SERVING SIZE: 1 BAR		PERCENT U.S. RDA PER SERVING	
CALORIES	210	PROTEIN	2%
PROTEIN	2g	VITAMIN A	*
CARBOHYDRATE	29g	VITAMIN C	*
FAT	10g	THIAMINE	4%
CHOLESTEROL	15mg	RIBOFLAVIN	2%
SODIUM	100mg	NIACIN	2%
POTASSIUM	60mg	CALCIUM	*
		IRON	2%

*Contains less than 2% of the U.S. RDA of this nutrient.

Lightly grease 8 or 9-inch square pan.* Arrange single layer of wafer cookies side by side over bottom of greased pan. Reserve half of wafer cookies for second layer. In small saucepan, melt caramels with milk over low heat, stirring occasionally until well blended. Spread evenly over wafer cookies in pan. Arrange reserved wafer cookies side by side in single layer over caramel mixture in pan. In small saucepan, melt chocolate chips with margarine over low heat, stirring occasionally. Spread evenly over wafer cookies. Cool until set. Cut into bars. 36 bars.

 MICROWAVE DIRECTIONS:

Lightly grease 8 or 9-inch square pan.* Arrange single layer of wafer cookies side by side over bottom of greased pan. Reserve half of wafer cookies for second layer. In medium microwave-safe bowl, combine caramels and milk. Microwave on MEDIUM for 3½ to 4 minutes or until caramels are melted, stirring once halfway through cooking. Stir until

smooth. Spread evenly over wafer cookies in pan. Arrange reserved wafer cookies side by side in single layer over caramel mixture in pan. In small microwave-safe bowl, combine chocolate chips and margarine. Microwave on MEDIUM for 2½ to 3½ minutes or until melted, stirring once halfway through cooking. Stir until smooth. Spread evenly over wafer cookies. Cool until set. Cut into bars.

TIP: * Size and shape of cookies will vary by brand. It will be necessary to experiment to determine if an 8 or 9-inch pan will work best and how to arrange the cookies to cover bottom of pan. In some cases, it will be necessary to cut a few cookies to fit.

NUTRITION INFORMATION PER SERVING

SERVING SIZE: 1 BAR		PERCENT U.S. RDA PER SERVING	
CALORIES	100	PROTEIN	*
PROTEIN	1g	VITAMIN A	*
CARBOHYDRATE	13g	VITAMIN C	*
FAT	5g	THIAMINE	*
CHOLESTEROL	2mg	RIBOFLAVIN	*
SODIUM	40mg	NIACIN	*
POTASSIUM	35mg	CALCIUM	*
		IRON	*

* Contains less than 2% of the U.S. RDA of this nutrient.

Each delectable bite bursts with the flavor of spiced candies. These bars are a perfect choice to serve with a cup of steaming fruit punch.

Spice Drop Bars

NUTRITION INFORMATION PER SERVING

SERVING SIZE: 1 BAR		PERCENT U.S. RDA PER SERVING	
CALORIES	150	PROTEIN	*
PROTEIN	1g	VITAMIN A	*
CARBOHYDRATE	29g	VITAMIN C	*
FAT	3g	THIAMINE	2%
CHOLESTEROL	20mg	RIBOFLAVIN	2%
SODIUM	45mg	NIACIN	*
POTASSIUM	50mg	CALCIUM	*
		IRON	4%

* Contains less than 2% of the U.S. RDA of this nutrient.

BARS

  1 cup firmly packed brown sugar
  1 tablespoon margarine or
      butter, softened
  1 tablespoon water
  2 eggs
  1 cup Pillsbury's BEST® All
      Purpose or Unbleached Flour
  ½ teaspoon cinnamon
  ¼ teaspoon salt
  1 cup coarsely chopped spiced
      gumdrop candies
  ¼ cup chopped nuts

FROSTING

    2 cups powdered sugar
    2 tablespoons margarine or
       butter, softened
2 to 3 tablespoons orange juice

Heat oven to 350°F. Grease 9-inch square pan. In large bowl, combine brown sugar and 1 tablespoon margarine; beat well. Add water and eggs; blend well. Lightly spoon flour into measuring cup; level off. Stir in flour, cinnamon and salt; mix well. Stir in candies and nuts. Spread in greased pan. Bake at 350°F. for 22 to 27 minutes or until light golden brown and top springs back when lightly touched in center. Cool completely.

In small bowl, combine all frosting ingredients, adding enough orange juice until frosting is of desired spreading consistency; beat until smooth. Spread over cooled bars. Cut into bars. 25 bars.

HIGH ALTITUDE — Above 3500 Feet: Increase flour to 1 cup plus 3 tablespoons. Bake as directed above.

Enjoy fall's abundance of zucchini by making these moist and satisfying bars. They have a comforting old-fashioned taste.

Zucchini Bars

BARS

    2 cups sugar
    ½ cup raisins
    ½ cup chopped nuts
    2 cups (3 medium) shredded
       zucchini
    1 cup oil
    1 teaspoon vanilla
    3 eggs
  2½ cups Pillsbury's BEST® All
       Purpose or Unbleached Flour
    1 teaspoon salt
    1 teaspoon cinnamon
    ½ teaspoon baking soda
    ½ teaspoon baking powder
    ½ teaspoon nutmeg
    ½ teaspoon cloves

FROSTING

    4 cups powdered sugar
3-oz. pkg. cream cheese, softened
    1 teaspoon vanilla
2 to 4 tablespoons milk

Heat oven to 350°F. Grease 15x10x1-inch jelly roll pan. In large bowl, combine sugar, raisins, nuts, zucchini, oil, vanilla and eggs; blend well by hand. Lightly spoon flour into measuring cup; level off. Stir in flour, salt, cinnamon, baking soda, baking powder, nutmeg and cloves; mix well by hand. Pour into greased pan. Bake at 350°F. for 25 to 35 minutes or until toothpick inserted in center comes out clean. Cool completely.

In large bowl, combine all frosting ingredients, adding enough milk until frosting is of desired spreading consistency; beat until smooth. Spread over cooled bars. Cut into bars. Store in refrigerator. 45 bars.

HIGH ALTITUDE—Above 3500 Feet: No change.

Delicate crumb layers that melt in your mouth surround a marvelous poppy seed filling. It's no wonder these bars were a favorite of our taste panel.

Poppy Seed Squares

FILLING
⅓ cup poppy seed, ground*
⅓ cup almonds, ground*
⅓ cup sugar
⅓ cup milk
2 tablespoons margarine or butter
½ teaspoon almond extract
1 egg white

BASE
1¾ cups Pillsbury's BEST® All Purpose or Unbleached Flour
¾ cup powdered sugar
⅓ cup ground almonds
1 teaspoon baking powder
¾ cup margarine or butter
1 teaspoon almond extract
1 egg yolk

To prepare filling, in small saucepan combine poppy seed, almonds, sugar and milk. Cook over medium heat 10 to 15 minutes or until thick and milk is absorbed. Cool 15 minutes. Stir in 2 tablespoons margarine, ½ teaspoon almond extract and egg white. Cool.

Heat oven to 350°F. Lightly spoon flour into measuring cup; level off. In medium bowl, combine flour, powdered sugar, ⅓ cup ground almonds and baking powder. Using pastry blender or fork, cut in ¾ cup margarine until mixture resembles coarse crumbs. With fork, stir in 1 teaspoon almond extract and egg yolk. Press half of crumb mixture firmly in bottom of ungreased 9-inch square pan. Carefully spread with filling mixture. Sprinkle with remaining crumb mixture; pat lightly. Bake at 350°F. for 25 to 33 minutes or until light golden brown. Cool completely. Cut into bars. 25 bars.

TIP: *Poppy seed and almonds can be ground in blender at medium speed for 1 minute, scraping sides once.

HIGH ALTITUDE—Above 3500 Feet: No change.

COOK'S NOTE

Baking Bars in Jelly Roll Pans

Follow specific recipe directions for baking pan sizes. Standard jelly roll pans are 15x10x1-inch. Using a jelly roll pan that does not have 1-inch sides may result in the recipe spilling over during baking.

◤◣ **POPPIN' FRESH® HOMEMADE COOKIES** ◤◣

This chewy cereal bar is chock-full of good things to eat. For a more festive holiday bar, use ½ cup each of red and green candied cherries.

Black Bottom Fruit and Nut Bars

6-oz. pkg. (1 cup) semi-sweet chocolate chips
¼ cup margarine or butter
4 cups slightly crushed cornflakes cereal
1 cup golden or dark raisins
1 cup chopped red candied cherries
¾ cup peanuts
14-oz. can sweetened condensed milk (not evaporated)

Heat oven to 350°F. Grease 13x9-inch pan. In small saucepan, melt chocolate chips and margarine over low heat, stirring occasionally. Spread evenly over bottom of greased pan. Refrigerate until set.

In large bowl, combine remaining ingredients until well coated. Press firmly over chocolate layer in pan. Bake at 350°F. for 17 to 20 minutes or until edges begin to bubble or top is lightly browned. Cool. Refrigerate until set. Cut into bars. Store in refrigerator. 36 bars.

NUTRITION INFORMATION PER SERVING
SERVING SIZE:
  BAR

		PERCENT U.S. RDA PER SERVING	
CALORIES	170	PROTEIN	4%
PROTEIN	3g	VITAMIN A	10%
CARBOHYDRATE	26g	VITAMIN C	6%
FAT	6g	THIAMINE	10%
CHOLESTEROL	4mg	RIBOFLAVIN	10%
SODIUM	160mg	NIACIN	10%
POTASSIUM	130mg	CALCIUM	4%
		IRON	4%

A flaky crust made from convenient and delicious refrigerated crescent dough is covered with tangy apricot preserves and a great-tasting coconut crumb topping.

Quick Crescent Hungarian Bars

8-oz. can Pillsbury Refrigerated Quick Crescent Dinner Rolls
1 cup chopped walnuts or almonds
¾ cup sugar
½ teaspoon cinnamon
¼ teaspoon nutmeg
10-oz. jar apricot or peach preserves

TOPPING
½ cup Pillsbury's BEST® All Purpose or Unbleached Flour
1 cup coconut
½ cup firmly packed brown sugar
¼ cup chopped walnuts or almonds
¼ cup margarine or butter, softened

Heat oven to 375°F. Separate dough into 2 long rectangles. Place in ungreased 13x9-inch pan; press over bottom to form crust. In medium bowl, combine 1 cup walnuts, sugar, cinnamon and nutmeg; sprinkle over crust. Drop teaspoonfuls of preserves evenly over nut mixture.

Lightly spoon flour into measuring cup; level off. In same bowl, combine all topping ingredients until crumbly; sprinkle over preserves. Bake at 375°F. for 20 to 27 minutes or until golden brown. Cool completely. Cut into bars. 36 bars.

NUTRITION INFORMATION PER SERVING
SERVING SIZE:
1 BAR

		PERCENT U.S. RDA PER SERVING	
CALORIES	130	PROTEIN	2%
PROTEIN	1g	VITAMIN A	*
CARBOHYDRATE	18g	VITAMIN C	*
FAT	6g	THIAMINE	2%
CHOLESTEROL	0mg	RIBOFLAVIN	*
SODIUM	70mg	NIACIN	*
POTASSIUM	60mg	CALCIUM	*
		IRON	2%

*Contains less than 2% of the U.S. RDA of this nutrient.

Black Bottom Fruit and Nut Bars

This moist, chewy coconut bar, reminiscent of a candy bar, is topped with whole almonds and drizzled with smooth and creamy chocolate.

Coconut-Almond Bars

4 egg whites
1½ cups sugar
1 tablespoon water
1 teaspoon almond extract
2 teaspoons vanilla
1 cup Pillsbury's BEST® All
   Purpose or Unbleached Flour
3 cups shredded coconut
48 whole almonds
½ cup semi-sweet chocolate chips
3 tablespoons margarine or butter

Heat oven to 350°F. Grease 15x10x1-inch jelly roll pan. In large bowl, beat egg whites until soft peaks form. Gradually add sugar; beat until stiff peaks form, about 7 minutes. Add water, almond extract and vanilla; blend well. Lightly spoon flour into measuring cup; level off. Stir in flour and coconut; mix well. Spread in greased pan. Arrange almonds over top of bars in 8 rows of 6 each. Bake at 350°F. for 15 to 20 minutes or until lightly browned and top springs back when lightly touched in center. Cover pan with foil until cool.

In small saucepan, melt chocolate chips and margarine over low heat, stirring occasionally; drizzle over cooled bars. Cut into bars. 48 bars.

HIGH ALTITUDE—Above 3500 Feet: Increase flour to 1¼ cups. Bake as directed above.

NUTRITION INFORMATION PER SERVING
SERVING SIZE:
1 BAR

	PERCENT U.S. RDA PER SERVING
CALORIES 90	PROTEIN . . . . *
PROTEIN 1g	VITAMIN A . . . . *
CARBOHYDRATE 12g	VITAMIN C . . . . *
FAT 4g	THIAMINE . . . . *
CHOLESTEROL 0mg	RIBOFLAVIN . . . . *
SODIUM 15mg	NIACIN . . . . *
POTASSIUM 40mg	CALCIUM . . . . *
	IRON . . . . *

*Contains less than 2% of the U.S. RDA of this nutrient.

Bran adds flavor, nutrition and texture to these extra good, down-home bars.

Bran Bars

1 cup sugar
½ cup margarine or butter, softened
¼ cup milk
1 teaspoon vanilla
2 eggs
1 cup Pillsbury's BEST® All Purpose
   or Unbleached Flour
½ cup shreds of bran cereal
½ teaspoon baking soda
¼ teaspoon salt
¼ cup raisins
   Powdered sugar

Heat oven to 350°F. Grease 9-inch square pan. In large bowl, beat sugar and margarine until light and fluffy. Add milk, vanilla and eggs; blend well. (Mixture will look curdled.) Lightly spoon flour into measuring cup; level off. Stir in flour, bran cereal, baking soda and salt; mix well. Spread in greased pan. Sprinkle raisins evenly over surface. Bake at 350°F. for 23 to 33 minutes or until toothpick inserted in center comes out clean. Cool completely. Sprinkle with powdered sugar. Cut into bars. 25 bars.

HIGH ALTITUDE—Above 3500 Feet: Decrease margarine to ⅓ cup; increase flour to 1⅓ cups. Bake as directed above.

NUTRITION INFORMATION PER SERVING
SERVING SIZE: PERCENT U.S. RDA
1 BAR   PER SERVING

	PERCENT U.S. RDA PER SERVING
CALORIES 100	PROTEIN 2%
PROTEIN 1g	VITAMIN A 4%
CARBOHYDRATE 14g	VITAMIN C . . . . *
FAT 4g	THIAMINE 2%
CHOLESTEROL 20mg	RIBOFLAVIN 2%
SODIUM 105mg	NIACIN 2%
POTASSIUM 40mg	CALCIUM . . . . *
	IRON 2%

*Contains less than 2% of the U.S. RDA of this nutrient.

Bran Bars

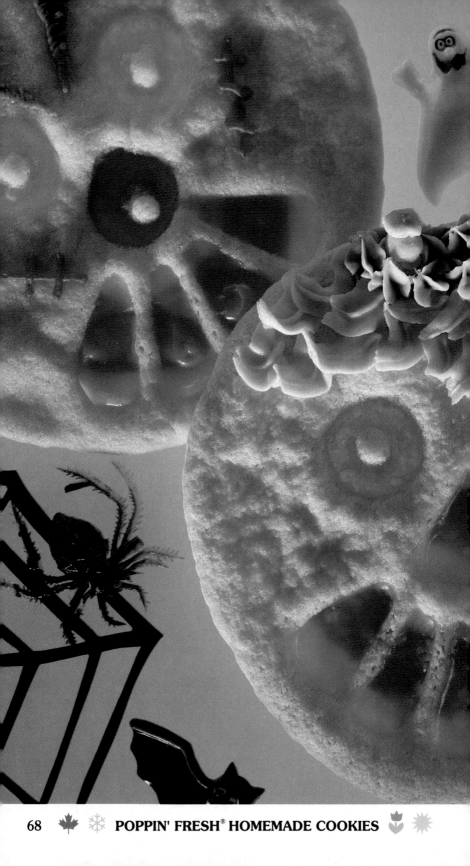

A
CALENDAR
OF
COOKIES

A CALENDAR OF COOKIES

To celebrate the seasons with special occasion cookies...

Winter, spring, summer, fall. What's the best cookie season of all? Why, all of them! The seasons provide a calendar of reasons—Chinese New Year, St. Patrick's Day, Mother's Day, Father's Day, the Fourth of July, Labor Day, Thanksgiving and of course, Christmas—to bake cookies. For the holidays big and small, and for the times of our lives, we've created special cookies to accompany them.

Celebrate Chinese New Year with homemade **Fortune Cookies**. Or make your own holiday in the midst of winter by cutting **Snowflakes** from tortillas and frying them to a golden brown. Send your sweetheart a bouquet of **Chocolate Valentine Cookies**. Press wooden skewers between the layers of these frosted sandwich cookies and add baby's breath and bows. It's a delectable way to say, "I love you."

Welcome spring on May Day with **White Chocolate May Baskets with Strawberry Cookies**. Neither the elegant, edible baskets nor the fruit-flavored morsels require baking. They're almost too beautiful to eat. Make Dad a card he'll never forget. **Father's Day Cookie Cards** start with the recipe for **Rolled Sugar Cookies**. Then, using a small paintbrush and colored evaporated milk, paint a design or write your own from-the-heart message. Holes punched in the "cards" let you tie two cookies together with colored ribbon or yarn.

For a high-flying summer, bake a **Lemon and Ginger Cookie Balloon**. The balloon and basket are baked and then spread with lemon frosting. String licorice forms the tethers. Just decorate and then up, up and away!

In a blink, summer's fading, the kids are heading back to school and the leaves begin to fall. Bring the colors of the season inside with **Almond Autumn Leaves**, leaf-shaped sugar cookies brushed with brilliant red and yellow. Spooky creatures haunt Halloween night. Keep them on their best behavior with **Peanut and Caramel Cookie Pops**. They're quick to fix, starting with refrigerated sugar cookie dough baked on sticks and then dipped into creamy caramel and chopped salted peanuts.

The first Thanksgiving feast included cranberries and pumpkin, new foods in a new world. **Cranberry-Pumpkin Bars** wed these two traditional flavors: a cranberry glaze glistening on moist, spicy pumpkin bars. Then Christmas, with its wealth of holiday cookies, completes the turn of the seasons. What better way to end the year!

Pictured on previous page: Crazy Cookie Creatures

What kind of creature can you create? Why not let your imagination run wild? These large, unique cookies are sure to be a hit with all those Halloween ghosts and goblins.

Crazy Cookie Creatures

20-oz. pkg. Pillsbury's BEST® Refrigerated Sugar Cookies
¼ cup sugar
4 (.90-oz.) pkg. fruit flavored, ring-shaped hard candies
Candy corn

FROSTING*

1 cup powdered sugar
1 tablespoon milk
1 tablespoon margarine or butter, softened
Food coloring

Heat oven to 350°F. Line cookie sheets with foil. Cut cookie dough into about twenty ½-inch slices. Shape each into ball; roll in sugar. Place 4 inches apart on foil-lined cookie sheets. With fingers, flatten into 4-inch circles, dipping fingers in sugar if necessary to prevent sticking. Firmly press ring-shaped candies in dough for eyes. Press candy corn in dough for ears, horns, teeth, beak or mouth to create desired creature. (Candies must be placed in dough, without extending beyond edge of dough.) Bake at 350°F. for 8 to 10 minutes or until edges are golden brown. Cool completely. Remove from foil.

In small bowl, combine powdered sugar, milk and margarine; blend until smooth. Add food coloring as desired. If necessary, add additional milk 1 drop at a time for desired piping consistency. Using pastry tube or knife, decorate cookies as desired. 20 cookies.

TIP: *Pillsbury Decorator Icing can be substituted.

NUTRITION INFORMATION PER SERVING

SERVING SIZE: 1 COOKIE		PERCENT U.S. RDA PER SERVING	
CALORIES	200	PROTEIN	°
PROTEIN	1g	VITAMIN A	°
CARBOHYDRATE	35g	VITAMIN C	°
FAT	6g	THIAMINE	4%
CHOLESTEROL	0mg	RIBOFLAVIN	4%
SODIUM	150mg	NIACIN	2%
POTASSIUM	15mg	CALCIUM	°
		IRON	4%

°Contains less than 2% of the U.S. RDA of this nutrient.

Tuck a special message inside these cookies to send in your child's lunch box. These simple-to-prepare cookies are sure to brighten your child's day. For an added surprise, dip the cookies in coconut or chopped peanuts or attach candy.

Secret Message Treats

6-oz. pkg. (1 cup) semi-sweet chocolate chips
30 square-shaped graham crackers

Melt chocolate chips in small saucepan over low heat, stirring constantly. Place one graham cracker on top of another; dip 3 sides in melted chocolate; allow excess to drip off.* Place on waxed paper until set. Prepare messages on 3 x 2-inch pieces of paper; fold lengthwise and slip in open end of cookie. (End of paper should remain visible outside of cookie.) 15 cookies.

▣ MICROWAVE DIRECTIONS:
In 2-cup microwave-safe measuring cup, microwave chocolate chips on MEDIUM for 2½ to 3½ minutes or until melted, stirring once halfway through cooking. Stir until smooth. Continue as directed above.

TIP: *For easier dipping, pour melted chocolate chips into shallow dish or pie pan.

NUTRITION INFORMATION PER SERVING

SERVING SIZE: 1 COOKIE		PERCENT U.S. RDA PER SERVING	
CALORIES	120	PROTEIN	2%
PROTEIN	2g	VITAMIN A	°
CARBOHYDRATE	17g	VITAMIN C	°
FAT	5g	THIAMINE	°
CHOLESTEROL	0mg	RIBOFLAVIN	6%
SODIUM	95mg	NIACIN	2%
POTASSIUM	90mg	CALCIUM	°
		IRON	4%

°Contains less than 2% of the U.S. RDA of this nutrient.

A tangy cranberry topping adds an interesting twist to these moist and spicy pumpkin bars. You may choose to eat them with a fork.

Cranberry-Pumpkin Bars

BARS
   2 cups Pillsbury's BEST® All Purpose or Unbleached Flour
   2 cups sugar
   2 teaspoons baking powder
   1 teaspoon baking soda
   2 teaspoons cinnamon
   ½ teaspoon salt
   1 cup oil
16-oz. can (2 cups) pumpkin
   4 eggs
   ½ cup chopped nuts
   ½ cup raisins

GLAZE
   2 cups powdered sugar
3 to 4 tablespoons water
   ½ cup cranberry juice cocktail
   2 teaspoons cornstarch

Heat oven to 350°F. Grease 15 x 10 x 1-inch jelly roll pan. Lightly spoon flour into measuring cup; level off. In large bowl, blend flour, sugar, baking powder, baking soda, cinnamon, salt, oil, pumpkin and eggs until moistened. Beat 2 minutes at medium speed. Stir in nuts and raisins. Pour into greased pan. Bake at 350°F. for 28 to 41 minutes or until toothpick inserted in center comes out clean. Cool completely.

In small bowl, combine powdered sugar and enough water until glaze is of desired spreading consistency; blend until smooth. Spread over cooled bars. In small saucepan, combine cranberry juice and cornstarch. Cook over medium-high heat until mixture boils and thickens, stirring constantly. Spoon cranberry mixture in horizontal par-

allel lines over top of glaze. Immediately draw knife through glaze in straight vertical lines to form pattern. 45 bars.

HIGH ALTITUDE — Above 3500 Feet: Increase flour to 2¼ cups. Bake as directed above.

NUTRITION INFORMATION PER SERVING

SERVING SIZE: 1 BAR		PERCENT U.S. RDA PER SERVING	
CALORIES	140	PROTEIN	2%
PROTEIN	1g	VITAMIN A	45%
CARBOHYDRATE	21g	VITAMIN C	*
FAT	6g	THIAMINE	2%
CHOLESTEROL	25mg	RIBOFLAVIN	2%
SODIUM	70mg	NIACIN	*
POTASSIUM	50mg	CALCIUM	*
		IRON	2%

*Contains less than 2% of the U.S. RDA of this nutrient.

These painted, leaf-shaped sugar cookies bake to the rich colors of autumn. Leaf-shaped cookie cutters are available in most kitchen specialty shops.

Almond Autumn Leaves

   1 cup sugar
   1 cup margarine or butter, softened
   3 tablespoons milk
   1 teaspoon almond extract
   1 egg, separated
   3 cups Pillsbury's BEST® All Purpose or Unbleached Flour
1½ teaspoons baking powder
   ½ teaspoon salt
   1 teaspoon water
   1 drop red food coloring
   1 drop yellow food coloring
      Sliced almonds, if desired

n large bowl, combine sugar, marga-
ine, milk, almond extract and egg white;
olend well. Lightly spoon flour into
measuring cup; level off. Stir in flour,
oaking powder and salt; mix well. Cover
with plastic wrap; refrigerate 1 hour
or easier handling. In small bowl, com-
oine egg yolk and water; blend well.
Divide into 2 small bowls. To one, stir
n yellow food coloring; to the other,
ed food coloring.

Heat oven to 400°F. On lightly floured
surface, roll dough, ½ at a time, to
⅛-inch thickness. Cut with floured
eaf-shaped cookie cutter. Place 1 inch
apart on ungreased cookie sheets.
Brush half of cookies with red egg yolk
mixture; brush remaining cookies with
yellow egg yolk mixture. Arrange
almonds on cookies. Bake at 400°F.
or 5 to 9 minutes or until edges are
ight golden brown. Immediately remove from cookie sheets. 4½ to
5 dozen cookies.

HIGH ALTITUDE — Above 3500 Feet:
ncrease flour to 3¼ cups. Bake as
directed above.

NUTRITION INFORMATION PER SERVING

SERVING SIZE: 1 COOKIE	PERCENT U.S. RDA PER SERVING	
CALORIES 70	PROTEIN	*
PROTEIN 1g	VITAMIN A	2%
CARBOHYDRATE 8g	VITAMIN C	*
FAT 4g	THIAMINE	2%
CHOLESTEROL 4mg	RIBOFLAVIN	2%
SODIUM 65mg	NIACIN	*
POTASSIUM 15mg	CALCIUM	*
	IRON	*

*Contains less than 2% of the U.S. RDA of this nutrient.

*These special treats can be made in
a flash with refrigerated sugar cookie
dough. The cookies are baked on a stick,
then topped with creamy caramel and
crunchy peanuts reminiscent of caramel
apples.*

Peanut and Caramel Cookie Pops

20-oz. pkg. Pillsbury's BEST®
    Refrigerated Sugar
    Cookies
  20 wooden sticks
   2 tablespoons milk
  24 vanilla caramels, unwrapped
   1 cup chopped salted peanuts

Heat oven to 350°F. Cut cookie dough
into about twenty ½-inch slices. Shape
each into ball. Arrange in circle on
ungreased cookie sheets, 3 inches
apart and 2 inches from edges. Securely
insert a wooden stick into each ball
with end pointing toward center of
cookie sheet. Bake at 350°F. for 10 to
14 minutes or until golden brown.
Cool 2 minutes; remove from cookie
sheet with spatula. Cool completely.

In small saucepan, melt caramels with
milk over low heat, stirring occasionally
until well blended. Cool 5 minutes.
Spread heaping teaspoon of caramel
on 1 side of cooled cookie; dip in
chopped peanuts. Repeat with remaining cookies. 20 cookie pops.

NUTRITION INFORMATION PER SERVING

SERVING SIZE: 1 COOKIE POP	PERCENT U.S. RDA PER SERVING	
CALORIES 210	PROTEIN	4%
PROTEIN 3g	VITAMIN A	*
CARBOHYDRATE 27g	VITAMIN C	*
FAT 10g	THIAMINE	6%
CHOLESTEROL 0mg	RIBOFLAVIN	6%
SODIUM 210mg	NIACIN	8%
POTASSIUM 85mg	CALCIUM	2%
	IRON	4%

*Contains less than 2% of the U.S. RDA of this nutrient.

Bake a batch of these special heart-shaped chocolate cookies with the creamy cherry filling for that special Valentine's Day party. For a unique gift or centerpiece, make a beautiful long-stemmed cookie bouquet as described in the tip below.

Chocolate Valentine Cookies

COOKIE
- 1 cup sugar
- 1 cup margarine or butter, softened
- ¼ cup milk
- 1 teaspoon vanilla
- 1 egg
- 2¾ cups Pillsbury's BEST® All Purpose or Unbleached Flour
- ½ cup unsweetened cocoa
- ¾ teaspoon baking powder
- ¼ teaspoon baking soda

FROSTING
- 2 cups powdered sugar
- ½ cup margarine or butter, softened
- Red food coloring
- 2 to 3 tablespoons maraschino cherry liquid or milk

In large bowl, beat sugar and 1 cup margarine until light and fluffy. Add milk, vanilla and egg; blend well. Lightly spoon flour into measuring cup; level off. Stir in flour, cocoa, baking powder and baking soda; mix well. Cover with plastic wrap; refrigerate 1 hour for easier handling.

Heat oven to 350°F. On floured surface, roll out dough, ⅓ at a time, to ⅛-inch thickness. Cut with floured 2½-inch heart-shaped cookie cutter. Place half of the cut-out hearts 1 inch apart on ungreased cookie sheets. Cut a 1-inch heart-shape from the centers of remaining hearts. Place cut-out hearts on cookie sheets. Cover and refrigerate remaining dough; reroll. Bake at 350°F. for 9 to 11 minutes or until set. Immediately remove from cookie sheets; cool.

In small bowl, combine all frosting ingredients, adding enough cherry liquid until frosting is of desired spreading consistency; blend until smooth. Frost bottom-side of whole cookie. Top with cut-out cookie. 4 dozen sandwich cookies.

TIP: To make a Valentine Heart Bouquet, prepare cookies as directed above. Press about 1½ inches of a 12-inch wooden skewer into frosting on bottom cookie. If necessary, spread additional frosting to cover skewer. Top with cut-out cookie. Refrigerate on cookie sheets for about 1 hour to set frosting. If desired, messages or designs can be added with decorator icing. Arrange bouquet in vase; add bows and baby's breath, if desired.

HIGH ALTITUDE—Above 3500 Feet: Decrease baking powder to ¼ teaspoon. Bake as directed above.

NUTRITION INFORMATION PER SERVING	
SERVING SIZE: 1 SANDWICH COOKIE	**PERCENT U.S. RDA PER SERVING**
CALORIES 110	PROTEIN . . . . *
PROTEIN 1g	VITAMIN A 4%
CARBOHYDRATE 14g	VITAMIN C . . . . *
FAT 6g	THIAMINE 2%
CHOLESTEROL 6mg	RIBOFLAVIN 2%
SODIUM 85mg	NIACIN 2%
POTASSIUM 20mg	CALCIUM . . . . *
	IRON 2%

*Contains less than 2% of the U.S. RDA of this nutrient.

What a fun idea for a Chinese New Year celebration or any occasion! By making your own fortune cookies you can create fortunes to fit the guests and/or occasion.

Fortune Cookies

1 egg
½ cup sugar
¼ cup margarine or butter, melted
1 teaspoon almond extract
⅔ cup Pillsbury's BEST® All
**   Purpose or Unbleached Flour**
⅛ teaspoon salt
⅓ cup milk

Prepare 36 fortunes on 2½ x ½-inch slips of paper.

Beat egg slightly in medium bowl. Add sugar, margarine and almond extract; mix well. Lightly spoon flour into measuring cup; level off. Stir in flour and salt. Add milk; stir until well blended.

Heat ungreased, non-stick surface electric skillet or crepe pan to 350°F. (medium-high heat). Spoon scant tablespoon of batter into skillet; quickly spread to a 3-inch circle.* Cook until deep golden brown, about 1 minute. Turn and cook other side for about 1 minute or until deep golden brown. Remove from skillet.

Working quickly, place cookie on clean folded towel. Place fortune in center of each cookie. Fold cookie in half to form semi-circle. Fold again over edge of bowl, points downward (see diagram). Place cookies in ungreased muffin cups to hold shape while cooling. After cookies are set, place on wire rack to cool completely. Store in airtight container at room temperature. 3 dozen cookies.

TIP: *If batter is too thick to spread, add 1 to 2 tablespoons additional milk.

HIGH ALTITUDE—Above 3500 Feet: No change.

NUTRITION INFORMATION PER SERVING

SERVING SIZE: 1 COOKIE		PERCENT U.S. RDA PER SERVING	
CALORIES	35	PROTEIN	°
PROTEIN	0g	VITAMIN A	°
CARBOHYDRATE	5g	VITAMIN C	°
FAT	1g	THIAMINE	°
CHOLESTEROL	8mg	RIBOFLAVIN	°
SODIUM	25mg	NIACIN	°
POTASSIUM	10mg	CALCIUM	°
		IRON	°

°Contains less than 2% of the U.S. RDA of this nutrient.

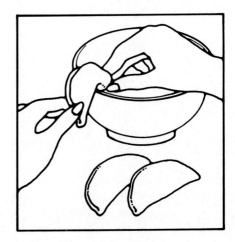

In this recipe, tortillas are folded and cut in the same way you would fold and cut paper snowflakes. Then they are fried into crisp, delicate pastries and sprinkled with powdered sugar.

Snowflakes

12 (6-inch) flour tortillas*
Oil for frying
Powdered sugar

Heat oven to 350°F.** Stack tortillas and wrap in foil. Heat at 350°F. for 7 minutes to soften. Fold each tortilla into fourths. With scissors, cut designs from folded edges; unfold.

In heavy skillet, heat ½ inch oil over medium heat.*** Fry 1 tortilla at a time 20 to 30 seconds on each side or until light golden brown. Drain on paper towels. Cool completely. Sprinkle with powdered sugar. Store in tightly covered container. 12 cookies.

TIPS: *Package sizes and diameters of tortillas vary. 7-inch tortillas can be substituted.

** To soften tortillas in microwave, place 6 tortillas in microwave-safe dish; cover with microwave-safe plastic wrap. Microwave on HIGH for 45 to 60 seconds or until softened.

*** The best temperature to fry tortillas is about 365°F.

Snowflakes

These feathery-light, fried pastries are traditionally sprinkled with sugar. For a more festive look these are dipped in colored icing.

Brightly Iced Rosettes

2 eggs
1 tablespoon sugar
¼ teaspoon salt
1 cup Pillsbury's BEST® All Purpose or Unbleached Flour
1 cup milk
¼ teaspoon vanilla
Oil for deep frying

ICING
1 cup powdered sugar
5 to 6 drops red, green or yellow food coloring
3 to 4 tablespoons milk

Beat eggs slightly in medium bowl. Add sugar and salt; blend well. Lightly spoon flour into measuring cup; level off. Add flour and 1 cup milk alternately, blending until smooth. Stir in vanilla.

In deep fryer or heavy saucepan, heat 3 to 4 inches oil to 365°F. Place rosette iron in hot oil for 30 to 60 seconds or until iron is hot. Gently dip hot iron into batter; DO NOT ALLOW TO RUN OVER TOP OF IRON. Return iron to hot oil, immersing completely for 25 to 30 seconds or until rosette is crisp and lightly browned.* Remove from oil; allow oil to drip off. Gently slip rosette off iron onto paper towel. Cool completely.

In small bowl, combine all icing ingredients, adding enough milk until icing is of desired dipping consistency; blend until smooth. (Mixture should be quite thin.) Gently dip top edges of rosettes (not rounded edges) into icing. Allow to dry, icing side up. Store in tightly covered container, making sure sides do not touch. 5 dozen rosettes.

TIP: *If rosettes drop from mold, oil is too hot. If rosettes are soft, increase frying time. If rosettes have blisters, eggs have been beaten too much.

HIGH ALTITUDE—Above 3500 Feet: No change.

NUTRITION INFORMATION PER SERVING

SERVING SIZE: 1 ROSETTE		PERCENT U.S. RDA PER SERVING	
CALORIES	60	PROTEIN	*
PROTEIN	1g	VITAMIN A	*
CARBOHYDRATE	4g	VITAMIN C	*
FAT	4g	THIAMINE	*
CHOLESTEROL	10mg	RIBOFLAVIN	*
SODIUM	15mg	NIACIN	*
POTASSIUM	10mg	CALCIUM	*
		IRON	*

*Contains less than 2% of the U.S. RDA of this nutrient.

A surprise cherry filling is spread over a golden brown crust and topped with a smooth, creamy frosting.

Maraschino Cherry Bars

CRUST
2 cups Pillsbury's BEST® All Purpose or Unbleached Flour
⅓ cup sugar
¾ cup margarine or butter, softened

FILLING
2 eggs, slightly beaten
1 cup firmly packed brown sugar
⅓ cup flour
1½ teaspoons baking powder
½ teaspoon salt
½ teaspoon vanilla
10-oz. jar maraschino cherries, drained, chopped, reserving liquid
½ cup chopped walnuts

FROSTING
2 tablespoons margarine or butter, softened
2½ cups powdered sugar
3 to 4 tablespoons reserved cherry liquid
3 to 4 tablespoons flaked coconut

Heat oven to 350°F. Lightly spoon flour into measuring cup; level off. In large bowl, combine all crust ingredients; blend at low speed until crumbly. Press mixture firmly in bottom of ungreased 13x9-inch pan. Bake at 350°F. for 12 to 15 minutes or until lightly browned. In large bowl, combine all filling ingredients; mix well. Spread evenly over partially baked crust. Return to oven and bake for an additional 15 to 25 minutes or until toothpick inserted in center comes out clean. Cool completely.

In small bowl, combine 2 tablespoons margarine, powdered sugar and cherry liquid, adding enough cherry liquid until frosting is of desired spreading consistency; beat until smooth. Spread over cooled bars; sprinkle with coconut. 36 bars.

HIGH ALTITUDE—Above 3500 Feet: Bake at 375°F. for 20 to 25 minutes.

NUTRITION INFORMATION PER SERVING

SERVING SIZE: 1 BAR		PERCENT U.S. RDA PER SERVING	
CALORIES	160	PROTEIN	2%
PROTEIN	2g	VITAMIN A	4%
CARBOHYDRATE	24g	VITAMIN C	*
FAT	6g	THIAMINE	4%
CHOLESTEROL	15mg	RIBOFLAVIN	2%
SODIUM	100mg	NIACIN	2%
POTASSIUM	55mg	CALCIUM	2%
		IRON	4%

*Contains less than 2% of the U.S. RDA of this nutrient.

Why not surprise a friend with these elegant, edible baskets filled with mouth-watering strawberry cookies? Neither the cookies nor the baskets require any baking.

White Chocolate May Baskets with Strawberry Cookies

12 oz. vanilla-flavored candy coating

COOKIES
3-oz. pkg. strawberry flavor gelatin
14-oz. pkg. (5⅓ cups) flaked coconut
14-oz. can sweetened condensed milk (not evaporated)
½ teaspoon almond extract
5 to 6 drops red food coloring, if desired

FROSTING*
1 cup powdered sugar
2 tablespoons margarine or butter, softened
1 tablespoon milk
3 to 4 drops green food coloring

Press foil firmly over outsides of six 5-oz. custard cups. Place cups in refrigerator.

In medium saucepan, melt candy coating over low heat, stirring constantly. Cool slightly. Pour into pastry bag with small writing tip. Drizzle coating randomly over bottom and sides of foil-covered cups, carefully connecting drizzled lines to prevent weak spots. Refrigerate until set. Unmold by carefully lifting foil from cups.** Carefully peel foil from candy coating. Place on tray. Refrigerate.

In large bowl, combine all cookie ingredients; blend well. Refrigerate 1 hour or until firm enough to handle. Using 1 tablespoon of cookie mixture for each cookie, form into strawberry shapes.

In small bowl, combine all frosting ingredients; beat until smooth. Using pastry bag and tips, pipe frosting stems and leaves on tops of strawberries. Allow frosting to set. Arrange 8 cookies in each basket. Store in refrigerator. 6 baskets; 4 dozen cookies.

TIPS: *If desired, green Pillsbury Decorator Icing can be substituted for frosting.

** If basket breaks, mend with melted candy coating.

NUTRITION INFORMATION PER SERVING

SERVING SIZE: 1 COOKIE		PERCENT U.S. RDA PER SERVING	
CALORIES	90	PROTEIN	2%
PROTEIN	1g	VITAMIN A	*
CARBOHYDRATE	13g	VITAMIN C	*
FAT	4g	THIAMINE	*
CHOLESTEROL	4mg	RIBOFLAVIN	2%
SODIUM	25mg	NIACIN	*
POTASSIUM	75mg	CALCIUM	2%
		IRON	*

*Contains less than 2% of the U.S. RDA of this nutrient.

NUTRITION INFORMATION PER SERVING

SERVING SIZE: 1 BASKET		PERCENT U.S. RDA PER SERVING	
CALORIES	310	PROTEIN	4%
PROTEIN	4g	VITAMIN A	*
CARBOHYDRATE	35g	VITAMIN C	*
FAT	17g	THIAMINE	*
CHOLESTEROL	10mg	RIBOFLAVIN	10%
SODIUM	50mg	NIACIN	*
POTASSIUM	170mg	CALCIUM	10%
		IRON	*

*Contains less than 2% of the U.S. RDA of this nutrient.

White Chocolate May Baskets with Strawberry Cookies

*These fun-to-make, festive cookies
burst with peppermint flavor. The shamrock is symbolic of St. Patrick's Day.
However, you can pipe on a different
design and serve these wonderful cookies
any time of the year.*

Chocolate-
Peppermint
Shamrock Cookies

1 cup sugar
½ cup shortening
½ teaspoon peppermint extract
3 oz. (3 squares) unsweetened
    chocolate, melted
2 eggs
1¾ cups Pillsbury's BEST® All
    Purpose or Unbleached Flour
¾ teaspoon baking soda
½ teaspoon salt
  Sugar

TOPPING

½ cup Pillsbury's BEST® All
    Purpose or Unbleached Flour
½ cup margarine or butter,
    softened
3 teaspoons warm water
4 drops green food coloring

In large bowl, beat 1 cup sugar and
shortening until light and fluffy. Add
peppermint extract, chocolate and
eggs; blend well. Lightly spoon flour
into measuring cup; level off. Stir in
1¾ cups flour, baking soda and salt;
mix well. Shape into 1-inch balls;
roll in sugar. Place 2 inches apart on
ungreased cookie sheets. Flatten with
bottom of glass dipped in sugar.

Heat oven to 375°F. Lightly spoon
flour into measuring cup; level off. In
small bowl, combine ½ cup flour, margarine and warm water; mix well. Stir
in food coloring. Spoon mixture into
pastry bag with small writing tip. Pipe
shamrock design on top of each cookie.
Bake at 375°F. for 6 to 10 minutes
or until set. 6 to 6½ dozen cookies.

HIGH ALTITUDE—Above 3500 Feet:
Increase flour to 1¾ cups plus 1 tablespoon. Bake as directed above.

NUTRITION INFORMATION PER SERVING

SERVING SIZE: 1 COOKIE		PERCENT U.S. RDA PER SERVING	
CALORIES	60	PROTEIN	*
PROTEIN	1g	VITAMIN A	*
CARBOHYDRATE	7g	VITAMIN C	*
FAT	3g	THIAMINE	*
CHOLESTEROL	6mg	RIBOFLAVIN	*
SODIUM	40mg	NIACIN	*
POTASSIUM	15mg	CALCIUM	*
		IRON	*

*Contains less than 2% of the U.S. RDA of this nutrient.

These cute little cookies are a sure reminder of spring.

Baby Bird Nest Cookies

½ cup firmly packed brown sugar
1 cup margarine or butter, softened
2 eggs, separated
1 teaspoon vanilla
2¼ cups Pillsbury's BEST® All Purpose or Unbleached Flour
½ teaspoon salt
1 cup coconut
¾ cup finely chopped nuts
  Corn syrup
  Tiny jelly beans or candy-coated chocolate pieces

Heat oven to 350°F. Lightly grease cookie sheets. In large bowl, beat brown sugar and margarine until light and fluffy. Add egg yolks and vanilla; blend well. Lightly spoon flour into measuring cup; level off. Stir in flour and salt; mix well. Shape dough into 1-inch balls. In small bowl, slightly beat egg whites. In separate small bowl, combine coconut and nuts. Dip balls in egg white, then in coconut-nut mixture. Place 1 inch apart on lightly greased cookie sheets. With end of wooden spoon or thumb, make indentation in center of each cookie.

Bake at 350°F. for 8 to 10 minutes or until edges are lightly browned. Cool 1 minute on cookie sheets. Remake indentations. Remove from cookie sheets; cool completely. Brush indentations lightly with corn syrup; fill with jelly beans. 4½ dozen cookies.

HIGH ALTITUDE—Above 3500 Feet: No change.

For a special touch of elegance, serve these crisp and airy morsels with a cup of tea. They would be perfect for Mother's Day.

Lemon Meringue Kisses

2 egg whites
2 teaspoons grated lemon peel
⅛ teaspoon salt
1 teaspoon lemon juice
⅔ cup sugar
1 tablespoon powdered sugar

Heat oven to 250°F. Cover cookie sheets with foil. In small bowl, beat egg whites, lemon peel, salt and lemon juice until foamy. Gradually add sugar; beat 3 to 5 minutes or until stiff peaks form. Fold in powdered sugar. Spoon mixture into pastry bag fitted with large fluted decorative tip with ½-inch opening. Pipe meringue kisses about 1½ inches in diameter 1 inch apart onto foil-lined cookie sheets. Bake at 250°F. for 50 to 60 minutes or until crisp and very lightly browned. Cool completely; remove from cookie sheets. 2½ to 3 dozen cookies.

HIGH ALTITUDE—Above 3500 Feet: Bake at 250°F. for 40 to 50 minutes.

No special pans are needed to create this lovable chocolate bunny.

Floppy-Eared Cookie Bunny

20-oz. pkg. Pillsbury's BEST® Refrigerated Chocolate Chocolate Chip or Chocolate Chip Cookies
Jelly beans or gumdrops
String licorice

Heat oven to 350°F. Line large cookie sheet (17x14-inch) with foil. Divide cookie dough in half; shape one half into large ball. To form bunny's body, press large ball into 8-inch circle 1 inch from bottom of foil-lined cookie sheet.* Divide remaining dough in half; shape one half into ball for bunny's head. Press into 5½-inch circle next to and slightly overlapping body. Divide remaining dough into 3 equal pieces; shape one third into small ball for bunny's tail. Flatten slightly next to and slightly overlapping body on lower left or right side. Shape remaining 2 pieces into floppy ears. Place on top of and slightly overlapping head. Decorate as desired using jelly beans for eyes, nose, mouth and buttons and string licorice for whiskers. Bake at 350°F. for 13 to 18 minutes or until set. Cool completely. Remove from foil. 20 servings.

TIP: *If dough becomes sticky, use floured hands to press dough out on cookie sheet.

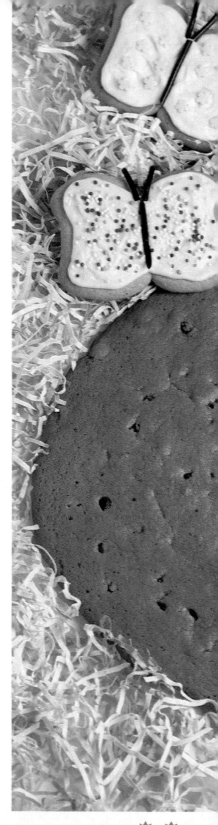

NUTRITION INFORMATION PER SERVING

SERVING SIZE: 1/20 OF RECIPE		PERCENT U.S. RDA PER SERVING	
CALORIES	140	PROTEIN	*
PROTEIN	1g	VITAMIN A	*
CARBOHYDRATE	22g	VITAMIN C	*
FAT	5g	THIAMINE	2%
CHOLESTEROL	0mg	RIBOFLAVIN	2%
SODIUM	65mg	NIACIN	2%
POTASSIUM	70mg	CALCIUM	*
		IRON	2%

*Contains less than 2% of the U.S. RDA of this nutrient.

Floppy-Eared Cookie Bunny and Butterfly Cookies p. 86

These delightful cookies are made with the convenience of Pillsbury's refrigerated cookie dough. Use your imagination to decorate these friendly creatures.

Butterfly Cookies

20-oz. pkg. Pillsbury's BEST®
   Refrigerated Sugar Cookies
1½ cups powdered sugar
   2 tablespoons margarine or
      butter, softened
2 to 3 tablespoons milk
4.5-oz. can Pillsbury Decorator
   Icing, if desired
   Multi-colored candy
      sprinkles or colored sugar
   String licorice

Heat oven to 350°F. Cut cookie dough into about thirty-six ¼-inch slices. Cut each slice in half. To form each butterfly, place 2 halves with rounded edges just touching on ungreased cookie sheet. Repeat with remaining cookie dough slices, placing 2 inches apart on ungreased cookie sheets. Bake at 350°F. for 7 to 11 minutes or until light golden brown. Immediately remove from cookie sheets. Cool completely.

In small bowl, combine powdered sugar, margarine and enough milk for desired spreading consistency. Beat until smooth. Spread over cooled butterfly cookies. Decorate as desired with decorator icing, candy sprinkles and string licorice. 3 dozen cookies.

NUTRITION INFORMATION PER SERVING
SERVING SIZE:
1 COOKIE

		PERCENT U.S. RDA PER SERVING
CALORIES	100	
PROTEIN	1g	PROTEIN .... *
		VITAMIN A .... *
CARBOHYDRATE	16g	VITAMIN C .... *
FAT	4g	THIAMINE 2%
CHOLESTEROL	0mg	RIBOFLAVIN 2%
SODIUM	75mg	NIACIN .... *
POTASSIUM	10mg	CALCIUM .... *
		IRON .... *

*Contains less than 2% of the U.S. RDA of this nutrient.

Surprise a father or grandfather with one of these personalized edible cards. Even small children can help paint pictures on the unbaked cookies.

Father's Day Cookie Cards

1 recipe unbaked Rolled Sugar
   Cookies (see Index)
¼ cup evaporated milk
   Food coloring

Prepare Rolled Sugar Cookie dough and refrigerate as directed in recipe. Divide evaporated milk into small bowls; color with food coloring.

Heat oven to 400°F. On lightly floured surface, roll dough, ½ at a time, into 16x12-inch rectangle. With pizza cutter, pastry wheel or sharp knife, cut dough into 6x4-inch rectangles. Place 1 inch apart on ungreased cookie sheets. Using small paintbrush and colored evaporated milk, paint desired designs or messages on unbaked cookies. Using drinking straw, punch holes in top or on 1 side of each rectangle. Bake at 400°F. for 6 to 8 minutes or until light golden brown. Cool 1 minute; remove from cookie sheets. Cool completely. To make cookie card, tie 2 cookies together with colored ribbon or yarn. 16 cookies (8 cards).

NUTRITION INFORMATION PER SERVING
SERVING SIZE:
1 COOKIE

		PERCENT U.S. RDA PER SERVING
CALORIES	250	PROTEIN 4%
PROTEIN	3g	VITAMIN A 10%
CARBOHYDRATE	31g	VITAMIN C .... *
FAT	12g	THIAMINE 10%
CHOLESTEROL	20mg	RIBOFLAVIN 6%
SODIUM	240mg	NIACIN 6%
POTASSIUM	50mg	CALCIUM 4%
		IRON 6%

*Contains less than 2% of the U.S. RDA of this nutrient.

Celebrate summer with this spicy cookie balloon complemented by a refreshing lemon frosting.

Lemon and Ginger Cookie Balloon

½ cup shortening
½ cup molasses
1½ cups Pillsbury's BEST® All
    Purpose or Unbleached Flour
1 teaspoon baking soda
½ teaspoon salt
¼ teaspoon ginger
⅛ teaspoon nutmeg
⅛ teaspoon cloves

FROSTING
2 cups powdered sugar
1 teaspoon grated lemon peel
¼ cup margarine or butter,
    softened
4 to 6 tablespoons milk

Multi-colored candy sprinkles
1 tablespoon semi-sweet
    chocolate chips, melted
Red or black string licorice

Heat oven to 350°F. Grease 9-inch round cake pan and 8x4-inch loaf pan. Line each with foil; grease foil. In large bowl, combine shortening and molasses; blend well. Lightly spoon flour into measuring cup; level off. Stir in flour, baking soda, salt, ginger, nutmeg and cloves; mix well by hand. With floured fingers, press about ⅓ of dough into bottom of greased, foil-lined loaf pan. Press remaining dough into bottom of greased, foil-lined cake pan. Bake at 350°F. for 8 to 12 minutes or until set. Cool completely. Remove from pans; remove from foil.

In small bowl, combine all frosting ingredients, adding enough milk until frosting is of desired spreading consistency; beat until smooth.

Cut rectangular cookie in half, forming 2 squares. Spread 2 tablespoons frosting over 1 square; top with second square. Position cookies on large serving tray or foil-covered cookie sheet, with 9-inch round cookie centered about 6 inches from square sandwich cookie. Frost tops and sides of cookies. Sprinkle candy sprinkles on round cookie. Drizzle melted chocolate chips in horizontal parallel lines on square cookie. Immediately draw knife through glaze in vertical lines to form pattern resembling basket weave.

Insert string licorice into cookie attaching bottom of round cookie to top of square cookie; poke holes in cookies with toothpick if necessary for ease in inserting licorice. 26 to 30 servings.

HIGH ALTITUDE—Above 3500 Feet: No change.

NUTRITION INFORMATION PER SERVING

SERVING SIZE: 1/30 OF RECIPE		PERCENT U.S. RDA PER SERVING	
CALORIES	120	PROTEIN	°
PROTEIN	1g	VITAMIN A	°
CARBOHYDRATE	17g	VITAMIN C	°
FAT	5g	THIAMINE	2%
CHOLESTEROL	0mg	RIBOFLAVIN	2%
SODIUM	95mg	NIACIN	2%
POTASSIUM	70mg	CALCIUM	2%
		IRON	2%

°Contains less than 2% of the U.S. RDA of this nutrient.

Serve these delightful cake-like bars as the patriotic finale to your 4th of July picnic.

Red, White and Blueberry Bars

BARS

     2 cups Pillsbury's BEST®
       All Purpose or
       Unbleached Flour
  1½ cups sugar
     2 teaspoons baking powder
     1 teaspoon salt
     1 cup milk
     ½ cup shortening
     4 egg whites
     ½ teaspoon almond extract
     1 cup fresh or frozen blueberries

FROSTING

     3 cups powdered sugar
     ¼ cup margarine or butter,
       softened
  3 to 5 tablespoons cherry liquid
       or milk
     ⅓ cup chopped maraschino
       cherries

Heat oven to 350°F. Grease 15x10x1-inch jelly roll pan. Lightly spoon flour into measuring cup; level off. In large bowl, blend flour, sugar, baking powder, salt, milk and shortening at low speed until moistened. Add egg whites and almond extract; beat 3 minutes at medium speed. Fold in blueberries. Pour into greased pan. Bake at 350°F. for 23 to 33 minutes or until toothpick inserted in center comes out clean. Cool completely.

In medium bowl, combine powdered sugar, margarine and enough cherry liquid until frosting is of desired spreading consistency; beat until smooth. Fold in cherries. Spread over cooled bars. 45 bars.

HIGH ALTITUDE—Above 3500 Feet: Increase flour to 2¼ cups. Bake as directed above.

Red, White and Blueberry Bars

NUTRITION INFORMATION PER SERVING
SERVING SIZE:
1 BAR

		PERCENT U.S. RDA PER SERVING	
CALORIES	110	PROTEIN	°
PROTEIN	1g	VITAMIN A	°
CARBOHYDRATE	19g	VITAMIN C	°
FAT	3g	THIAMINE	2%
CHOLESTEROL	0mg	RIBOFLAVIN	2%
SODIUM	80mg	NIACIN	°
POTASSIUM	25mg	CALCIUM	°
		IRON	°

°Contains less than 2% of the U.S. RDA of this nutrient.

These bars are unbelievably easy to make and unbelievably irresistible to eat. They are an ideal choice for days when it's too hot to use the oven.

No-Bake Bars

     2 cups sugar
     ¼ cup unsweetened cocoa
     ½ cup milk
     ½ cup margarine or butter
     1 cup peanut butter
     1 teaspoon vanilla
     2 cups quick-cooking rolled oats
     1 cup shredded coconut

Lightly grease 13x9-inch pan. In large saucepan, combine sugar, cocoa, milk and margarine. Bring to a boil over medium heat, stirring constantly; remove from heat. Add peanut butter and vanilla; mix well. Stir in rolled oats and coconut. Spread in greased pan. Refrigerate until set. Cut into bars. Store in refrigerator. 36 bars.

◨ MICROWAVE DIRECTIONS:
Lightly grease 13x9-inch pan. Place margarine in 2-quart microwave-safe bowl. Microwave on HIGH for 60 seconds or until melted. Stir in sugar, cocoa and milk; mix well. Microwave on HIGH for 3½ to 4½ minutes or until mixture boils, stirring once halfway through cooking. Continue as directed above.

NUTRITION INFORMATION PER SERVING
SERVING SIZE:
1 BAR

		PERCENT U.S. RDA PER SERVING	
CALORIES	140	PROTEIN	4%
PROTEIN	3g	VITAMIN A	2%
CARBOHYDRATE	17g	VITAMIN C	°
FAT	7g	THIAMINE	2%
CHOLESTEROL	0mg	RIBOFLAVIN	°
SODIUM	70mg	NIACIN	4%
POTASSIUM	85mg	CALCIUM	°
		IRON	2%

°Contains less than 2% of the U.S. RDA of this nutrient.

NUTRITION INFORMATION

Pillsbury's NUTRI-CODED system can help you in your daily food planning. Below are guidelines:

SERVING SIZE: This has been determined as a typical serving for each recipe.

CALORIES: The amount of calories a person needs is determined by age, size and activity level. The recommended daily allowances generally are: 1800-2400 for women and children 4 to 10 years of age and 2400-2800 for men.

PROTEIN: The amount of protein needed daily is determined by age and size; the general U.S. RDA is 65 grams for adults and children of at least 4 years of age.

CARBOHYDRATE, FAT, CHOLESTEROL, SODIUM, AND POTASSIUM: Recommended Daily Allowances (RDA) for these nutrients have not been determined; however, the carbohydrate should be adequate so the body does not burn protein for energy. The American Heart Association recommendation for those who wish to restrict dietary cholesterol is for a daily intake that is less than 100 milligrams per 1000 calories and not exceeding a total of 300 milligrams.

PERCENT U.S. RDA PER SERVING: For a nutritionally balanced diet, choose recipes which will provide 100% of the U.S. Recommended Daily Allowance for each nutrient.

Pillsbury Guidelines for Calculating the Nutrition Information:

- When the ingredient listing gives one or more options, the first ingredient listed is the one analyzed.
- When a range is given for an ingredient, the larger amount is analyzed.
- When ingredients are listed as "if desired," these ingredients are included in the nutrition information.
- Serving suggestions listed in the ingredients are calculated in the nutrition information.
- When each bread recipe is analyzed, a serving of yeast-leavened bread is a 1-oz. slice and a quick bread serving is $1/16$ of the loaf. Recipes that vary are indicated.

Symbol Meanings:

The following symbols are used in relation to the nutrition data:

*   Less than 2% of the nutrient
<1   Less than one gram (or milligram) of the nutrient

Any questions regarding nutrition information in this book should be addressed to:

The Pillsbury Company
Pillsbury Center — Suite 2866
Minneapolis, Minnesota 55402

The primary source for values used in this program is the revised Agriculture Handbook No. 8. The values are only as correct and complete as the information supplied.

NOTE FOR PEOPLE WITH SPECIAL DIETARY NEEDS: CONSULT YOUR PHYSICIAN REGARDING RELIANCE ON THE NUTRITION INFORMATION IN THIS BOOK. Every effort has been made to ensure the accuracy of this information. However, The Pillsbury Company does not guarantee its suitability for specific medically imposed diets.

INDEX

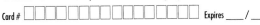